First Edition published 2022

Printed and bound in Great Britain by

www.elitepublishingacademy.com

A catalogue record for this book

is available from The British Library

ISBN Paperback - 978-1-915730-10-7

Pet Business Marketing Magic

The secrets to transform your boring, bashful, broke business into a brilliant, bold, booming beast of an operation

By Dominic Hodgson

<u>What pet professionals are saying about Pet Business Marketing Magic</u>

"A literal 'How To' book on creating magical experiences for your clients. Step-by-step processes, outlined for your use.

While this book is written for pet business owners, every business should be listening to Dominic.

Dominic is one of those rare coaches that practises what he preaches.

This book reads like Dominic personally interviewed Walt Disney himself!"

Vance Morris
Disney Customer Service Expert

"As a fan of both Disney and Dom, I was excited to read this book and was not disappointed. It breaks down the Disney secrets to success and shows you how to apply these powerful principles to grow your pet business.

Read it, take the actions steps and create your own magic for your customers and your business."

Fernando Camacho
Overdog Digital

"Dom Hodgson does it again. This book clearly explains how you can be Tinkerbell to your own business and sprinkle magic dust all over it. These suggestions will help make anyone's business stand out from the rest and be successful. They are clear suggestions that have been proven to work many times before.

Don't be like Grumpy from Snow White and think it's all a gimmick – buy the book and be the success you always wanted to be."

Tony Sherry
ECH Therapies

"This book is a must read. I sat down to read a chapter or two and read the whole thing in one sitting, and that's coming from someone who normally takes forever to read a book, especially a business book.

It's practical, easy-to-action advice that, if applied, really will add the fairy dust sparkle to your business both for you and your customers. I now have a longer to-do list, and it's given me a kick up the arse to finish some of those items I'd started and get them out into the world. Thank you, Dom.

It's also come at just the right time for the birth of my next business (ad)venture, so fairy dust will be sprinkled on that one as well."

Sara Barnes
Owner & Founder
Who Lets Your Dog Out?

'What can I say, other than it's magic!

For a slim book, Pet Business Marketing Magic is absolutely bursting at the seams with business brilliance.

There are so many snippets about how to raise your business game to the next professional level, while being sprinkled throughout with Disney magic and 'Dom humour'.

Dom's enthusiasm for customer service and ensuring client satisfaction, and therefore client retention, is apparent from the get-go… even the strapline makes you sit up, take notice, and want to get on board the Disnifying Railroad.

With advice on systems, onboarding, storytelling, and marketing, I have no doubt that this little book will be your 'go-to for inspiration' guidebook – I know it's certainly going to be mine.

Lez Graham
The Pet Gundog Club

'Wow! I read Pet Business Marketing Magic cover to cover in one sitting, and it is the most straightforward guide to building a rock star pet business I have ever seen.

As usual, Dom tells it exactly how it is with his humorous no-bullshit writing style. There is no reason you shouldn't have the business of your dreams after reading this. I only wish Dom had written this years ago!

I have already implemented a lot of what Dom writes about in this book in my pet business and am ready to 'plus it' all after reading this! Every pet business owner, new or veteran, should read this book and think about how you can 'plus' your business!"

Doug Keeling
Owner & Founder of Bad to the Bone Pet Care

"From Dumbo to Maleficent, there's magic to be found in the wisdom of Disney. Dominic lays out simple truths for pet business owners to wow their clients, set themselves apart, and make their business irresistible to the exact clients they want.

In a way only Dominic can, he presents practical, hard-hitting business know-how alongside Peter Pan and Goofy that will leave you motivated to start bringing the magic to your business and clients."

Collin & Meghan Funkhouser
Pet Sitter Confessional Podcast

"When I heard the title of Dom's new book: 'Pet Business Marketing Magic' I was instantly intrigued and excited...

I've always been a big fan of Disney; I've got the T-shirts, the plush toys and even enjoyed running races dressed as Disney characters!

What I really liked was how Dom was able to create a book that took the joy, excitement and WOW factor of Disney and turn this into a model for ambitious pet owners to help build or expand upon their business. All the things pet business owners may fear – including premium pricing, upsells and doing things a little differently (which work!).

I found the book relatable, fun (with Dom's wittiness added) and not just another marketing book. Plus I learnt so much I didn't know about Disney in a non-goofy way ;). Win, win!"

Helen Motteram
Social Paws Cheltenham
Pet Professional Network

"DONT BUY THIS BOOK!!

You are happy as you are, you don't need to improve your business – nothing to see here, this is not the book you're looking for!

All joking aside, if you have a pet business you NEED this book, it has lots of great but simple ideas that you can put into your business straight away and some that you can develop further along your business journey.

A straight-talking, no-nonsense book sprinkled with some Disney inspiration.

If you only buy one book to help you with your business, then it should be this one!

I can see this being my favourite of Dom's books that he has written so far. While it's a short book and I read it in two sessions, it doesn't hold back on the information inside, with Dom's no-nonsense approach sprinkled with some Disney magic.

So, for Disney lovers like myself, it is a real treat to have some business fundamentals tied together with some fairy dust.

The chapters concentrate on different areas that you can quickly adapt to your business to go from run-of-the-mill to standout.

Even if you only take one of the ideas from the book, you will see a positive effect on your business.

I have been implementing a few of the ideas for a while now and have seen great results. I am really enjoying my business again, not dreading the day to day with rubbish customers."

Allison Pearson
The Stress Free Groomer

"I have had the pleasure of reading all of Dom's books. This book is the best one yet!

Packed with entertaining stories and ideas that you won't find anywhere else.

You can implement them straight into your business to 'wow' your clients and make you stand out while increasing your bank balance. Thank you Dom for an enjoyable read!"

Harriet Goodall
Teenage Gundog Tamer

"Generous pet professionals will love this book!

I've just had a lightbulb moment when I realised why I love this book so very much… and if you're a generous pet professional, you're going to love it too.

There's an endemic in the dog care industry… we turn ourselves inside out overdelivering and undervaluing ourselves. Would you agree? Before working with Dom, I was guilty of this too .

What I absolutely love about this little cracker of a book is that it outlines how to be generous and how to overdeliver to create a magical experience for our clients, while valuing and rewarding ourselves properly for our exceptional efforts.

As you would expect from the King of Canine Common Sense – even when he does Disney – the formula is crystal clear and straightforward enough that you'll be able to begin implementing it straightaway.

While everyone else is running from the recession, we'll be plussing it. Join us?"

Katie Guastapaglia
Dogwood Adventure Play
Scentventure

"Dom's enthusiasm and excitement for building pet business shouts out from every page. A great condensed view of the massive Disney enterprise and simply but expertly applied to pet businesses. Straight to the point.

If you work with pets, and want to wow with your services, read this book."

Michelle Cleary
Cleary Canines

"I've been a fan of Dom's work for years, and there's no doubt his ideas have massively increased the success of my business.

This new book might be his best yet. Seamlessly combining the principles that made him a famous pet business coach with the experience-driven mindset that makes Disney such an iconic brand."

Nick Benger
Hound+

Pet Business Marketing Magic

A personal note from the author, and a special book buyer's bonus…

Dear Pet Business Owner;

Thanks for buying my book. You are in for a life-changing experience.

To reward you for investing in your pet business education, I have a special bonus that will help you move forward faster with your business growth.

I've recorded an exclusive audio version of this book, which is packed with bonus material, examples and case studies that back up the proven marketing secrets I share in *Pet Business Marketing Magic.*

To get immediate access to this valuable resource go to:

www.petbusinessmarketing.com/magicgift

Warmly

Dom Hodgson
The Pet Biz Wiz
www.petbusinessmarketing.com

Contents

Preface

How Good Do You Want To Be?

'Venture outside your comfort zone. The rewards are worth it.'

Rapunzel

Before I entered the pet industry in 2011, I worked as a sales representative for Imperial Tobacco.

After about five years in the role and numerous failed promotion attempts, the management picked a bunch of us to attend an assessment weekend at a place called Swallet Farm, near Bristol.

This was no ordinary assessment.

This was an outdoor adventure experience with group bonding activities, outdoor trails and problem-solving exercises, where we would be tested physically, mentally and emotionally, to see which of us was worthy of consideration to become…wait for it…a Regional Account Manager.

Heady stuff, I don't mind telling you.

Imagine Bear Grylls meets *The Apprentice*, plus me in a Marks and Spencer's pinstripe suit and you'll get the idea.

Now, lots of people roll their eyes with this type of corporate development stuff, but I'm always game for a laugh, and I love trying new things, so I was pretty delighted to be picked to attend the assessment.

And do you know what, dear reader?

I absolutely smashed it.

Seriously, though…I really did.

Or I *thought* I did anyway.

I certainly tried everything that was asked of me, and never shirked a challenge. I mucked in with the cooking and cleaning *and* tried to help those who were struggling a bit, who were missing their loved ones at home.

And what did I achieve for my sterling efforts?

Absolutely sod all.

Nothing.

Zilch.

Nada.

Zip.

I didn't get so much as an interview for any of the promotion opportunities on offer.

Now, it could be I was totally unsuited to the role, but I somewhat resented not being given what I felt was a fair crack of the whip.

I remember having a post-assessment debrief with my Regional Manager. He basically read down the list of competencies, most of which I thought I'd hit or exceeded, and then gave me some mealy-mouthed bollocks about it being 'not quite my time'.

This phrase sticks in my mind vividly: *'The opportunities are there Dom, but you've got to come to the party.'*

I was sat there thinking *'Come to the party??? I am the party, you dingus. I'm DJing, I'm prepping canapes and serving drinks for everyone!'*

That was probably the beginning of the end of my tenure at Imperial, although with hindsight it was also probably the best thing that ever happened to me.

It's funny how some of life's disappointments turn out later to be a blessing in disguise.

Because, even though I didn't know what I was going to do when I left Imperial, I had a strong sense that I needed to do something else, where all my efforts would be recognised and rewarded.

I HATE being put in a box by anyone else.

I HATE being told I can't do anything.

I HATED having my future dictated to me by people who were, in my humble, honest and accurate opinion, often less competent than me.

So, yeah, maybe I wasn't cut out to be a good employee.

However, starting and running my own pet business meant the shackles were finally off.

No more would my progress be dependent on the whims and wants of someone above me.

This business was my baby, and I was 110% focused on blowing my competition completely out of the water.

Yes sirree, when I started my pet business I was determined to 'Be the Best'.

That might sound big-headed for someone who, at the time, knew nothing about running a dog business, but I figured I knew enough to get started, and I could learn the rest as I went along. In the meantime, all I had to do was beat the competition, and there was no way I was going to be beaten by that sorry lot.

I'd beat them on price (by charging more).

I'd beat them on service (by offering and delivering a better experience).

I'd beat them with my marketing (by working smarter *and* harder to sell my superpowers).

I'd beat them all ends up, 7 days a week – and twice on Sundays – 365 days a year.

And ultimately that's what I did.

I'm sure you started your pet business with a similar intention.

To be, and be known as, the best pet business in town.

That decision you make to be the best is crucial to your success.

When I was working as a cigarette rep, I met all kinds of shopkeepers. Many had inherited their business, or used a redundancy payment to quit their job and be their own boss.

However, lots of these people ended up hating their lives.

The truth is, they were rubbish business owners with no enthusiasm or plan for success, who did nothing but moan about the economy, their customers or their bad luck in life.

But there was a small handful of renegade shopkeepers who were smashing it out of the park.

They were always busy, always selling something, always lively and engaging with their customers.

The location of the shop had a lot to do with their success, but I saw many people take a run-down shop, expand it, add services, build it up, sell it and then invest in a better location where they could repeat the process.

Basically, these people decided what they were going to achieve, they put a plan in place and then worked their nuts off to make it happen.

That's what I did with my business, and it's what you get to decide to do with your pet business.

You get to decide whether you want to be the best in your town.

Or the best in your field.

Or the best in the world.

Instead of good.

Or quite good.

Or OK.

Did you really quit your job to start an OK pet business that brings enough money in for you to get by?

I didn't think so.

So, why not sets your sights a bit, or a LOT, higher?

I bet you already have the drive and determination to succeed. All you're lacking is a plan to take your pet business to the next level.

Well, that proven plan is *exactly* what you'll get with Pet Business Marketing Magic.

Let's start with a grand vision for where you want to take your business.

Walt Disney was also a man of vision, who was not prepared to put up with second best in any of the projects he worked on.

So, before we start sprinkling some marketing magic, let's begin our Disney deep-dive by seeing how you can start doing things the Walt Disney Way.

Introduction

The Disney Way

'Disneyland is a show.'

Walt Disney

In the mid-2000s, my cousin took his wife and two daughters to Disneyland, Orlando, five years in a row.

My wife Beth and I used to roll our eyes and say, *'How boring and unimaginative! Are they going there again? Surely, it can't be that good…Isn't there somewhere else* IN THE *WORLD they could visit???'*

Then a couple of years later when our two boys were big enough, we booked our first trip to Disney Orlando…and we were so blown away we booked up to go straight back the following year.

Total hypocrites, I know!

We'll be talking a lot about the 'Disney Magic' over the next six chapters, and whether that phrase makes you want to barf all over the floor or wee yourself with excitement, you can't deny that from a business point of view, it makes sense to study, and copy, the marketing methods of a company that can turn the hardest of sceptics into raving fans.

These super-fans keep coming back year after year, and they also become recruitment officers who tell others about the amazing experience they had at Disney.

Now, wouldn't it be amazing if your pet business was known in your town as the Disney of dog walking, dog training, dog grooming, or doggy day care?

Where would we start with such a process?

Walt Disney himself said , *'Whatever you do, do it well. Do it so well that when people see you do it, they will want to come back and see you do it again, and they will want to bring others and show them how well you do what you do.'*

That's the Disney way, and the first step to creating 'word of mouth' marketing.

Being fucking awesome.

Walt Disney's greatest skill wasn't invention, it was iteration, i.e., taking things that already exist and improving them and making them so good that people would be prepared to pay more money to experience what **he** was offering.

Walt didn't invent cartoons, but the Mickey Mouse debut cartoon *Steamboat Willie* is notable for being the first Disney cartoon with synchronised sound.

He took an existing concept and made it a better experience.

Then, when everyone else was making cartoon shorts, he took the concept further and created the full-length animated movie, *Snow White*.

When he made *Bambi*, he improved the animation process by creating a small zoo on set so the animators could learn to draw realistic-looking animals.

He did this with theme parks too.

Legend has it he was turned off by the vulgarity and grime he found when he went to other amusement parks.

Disney's goal was to create a park where parents and children could have fun together.

He visited a number of amusement parks, from Tivoli Gardens in Copenhagen (which I've been to and can definitely see how it inspired the look of the Magic Kingdom), to Griffith Park in Los Angeles. Griffith Park was a modest but clean little amusement park with a merry-go-round, a waterless boat ride (the boats moved on wheels), and a small train that ran around the park.

Legend has it that Walt sat on a bench, occasionally asking the children which rides they enjoyed the most.

This led to the creation of Disneyland, in Anaheim, California, in 1955.

This brings us to the first – and main – takeaway from this book:

For you to have a standout, successful pet business, you ***don't*** need to create a brand new 'thing' that's never been done before.

You don't need a unique service that no-one currently offers.

You don't need a more expensive whizzbang website with moving pictures and wonderful SEO.

You don't need to waste time writing 1,000 blogs about why dogs shouldn't eat conkers or chocolate.

In fact, it can be pretty dangerous to try and come up with a totally unique way of doing things. If you are successful then someone is going to copy you, eventually.

No, all you need to do to be hugely successful is take your existing business and make sure that it is WAY better than your competition.

That's the secret to Disnifying your pet business, and adding Marketing Magic to your operation.

Walt did this continually throughout his business journey.

This concept became known as 'plussing'.

He always asked, 'How can we take an experience and 'plus' it for the customer?'

A key component of 'plussing' is exceeding customer's expectations. Here's an example:

Shortly after Walt Disney opened his first theme park, he decided to hold a Christmas parade. When he totalled up the expense, he realised his idea and vision would cost the park roughly $350,000.

His accountants begged him not to spend the money because the people would already be there and nobody would complain if it didn't happen as no one was expecting it.

Disney's response was,

'We should do it precisely because no one's expecting it. Our goal at Disneyland is to always give people more than they expect. As long as we keep surprising them, they'll keep coming back. But if they ever stop coming, it'll cost us ten times that much to get them to come back.'

So, to Disnify an experience is to 'plus' it.

And you can Disnify your pet business by 'plussing' everything about it so you quickly overtake – and remain – streets ahead of your competition.

The great news is that it isn't too difficult to do, because the competition in your town will be offering more of a slapdash Mr Smee shitshow of a service than a magical, marvellous Mary Poppins Experience (*practically perfect in every way, geddit?*).

That word 'experience' is key to making this happen.

At every stage of your customer journey, you need to find ways to 'WOW' your prospects and clients.

See, Disney are in the business of creating an 'experience' for their customers.

And not just any experience.

A once-in-a-lifetime 'Disney' experience.

You see, rides, candyfloss and people dressed up as animals, Disney can get anywhere.

Most medium-sized towns in the Western world still have a two-week period when the travelling circus or fairground arrives. Some people love these carnivals and look forward to them all year. Personally, I'd rather wash my hair in a bucket of dog vomit than spend time with a load of cheapskates who are looking for cheap thrills on tin-pot merry-go-rounds, but each to their own.

It's an experience for sure. But it's not one I want to take part in.

Well, Disney thought the same and right from the beginning, he decided his theme park would be an unmatched experience in every way from anything that already existed.

See, you can only get a Disney experience at Disney.

Similarly, dog owners in your town can get dog walks, haircuts, training and day care from anyone with a Facebook page, some leads, scissors, a van, a unit and a pocketful of treats…

…but they can only get your unique 'WOW Factor'-filled Disney-like experience from YOU.

Your task is to make that experience a reality, and that's what this book will help you do.

Over the course of the next six short chapters, we'll be looking at how Disney villains can help you attract the perfect client, how to implement Disney-style pricing and promotions, and how to use Imagineering and creativity to create standout services.

However, we're starting with me showing you how to create a Disney level of customer service in your pet business.

This ties in with one of Disney's founding principles – storytelling – and specifically which stories you want people to tell about your business.

What do you want your pet business to be known for?

Disneyland is known as *'The happiest place on Earth'*.

Now, that's a pretty ballsy statement, don't cha' think?

How did this happen?

Well, it wasn't because the branding fairy appeared one day and granted Disney permission to call themselves 'The happiest place on earth'.

Disney gave themselves that label, and everyone who works there is aligned with making the vision a reality.

So, my little Minnie Mouse, I have a question for you:

What does your pet business stand for?

What do you want to be known for?

What do you want to be known as?

Here's an interesting idea…

Why not want to be known as the best, most amazing, exclusive and expensive, affluent-attracting, most caring, talented, helpful, customer-centric pet business in your town?

All this starts with a decision by you.

Today!

It's not about how much experience you have, or the type of people in your town, or how well the economy is doing, or how much competition you have.

It's about YOU deciding 'This is what I'm going to be known for!'

Advertising legend Paul Arden said: *'Your vision of where or who you want to be is the greatest asset you have. Without having a goal it's difficult to score.'*

So, let's start this journey by setting your sights a little (or a LOT) higher.

Let's create some aspirational goals for your business that match your ambition.

See, your pet business is going to be known for *something.*

You are going to acquire a reputation for *something.*

Whether you set the narrative or not, there **will** be stories told about your business.

So, why not do everything you can to ensure that the stories being told are worthy of a Disney blockbuster?

What stories are your clients telling about you right now?

How you 'WOW' your customers this week will influence the stories they tell about you next week.

That's how you build a reputation that has you feared and revered by your competitors.

Disnifying your pet business is about taking the ordinary and making it extraordinary.

And adding WOW Factor, which is the subject of Chapter One…

Chapter One

How to Add 'WOW' Factor to Your Pet Business

'What do you want me to do? Dress in drag and do the hula?'

Timone

First of all, let's dive into exactly what the WOW Factor is.

The Cambridge Dictionary defines it as:

'…a quality or feature of something that makes people feel great excitement or admiration…'

'Wow' is an exclamation of astonishment. And to 'astonish' is to surprise greatly.

So, by adding the WOW Factor we are really talking about making your clients 'feel' something.

We want them to *feel* excitement.

We want them to admire, approve, appreciate and even adore what you do for them.

And to surprise and create excitement, anticipation and astonishment means you need to surprise every prospect and client who comes into your world.

How do you surprise your clients?

Well, you don't dress up as Goofy, sneak up behind them and shout *'Boo baby!'* next time you see them.

No.

That would be silly.

You want to give your prospects and clients a 'good surprise'.

A surprise is defined as an unexpected event, and *to surprise* is to cause feeling of wonder and amazement.

That might sound a tall order, but it's very doable, and I'll show you how in this chapter.

To create these feelings of wonder and excitement, you essentially need to 'up' the experience at every touch point that exists with a client or prospect.

As part of my research for this book I interviewed a good pal of mine, Vance Morris.

Vance is a former Disney Customer Service Leader, and he has helped hundreds of businesses in all kinds of industries to implement a Disney-standard customer service. In fact, you could say there's not much Vance '*disney*' know about Disney customer service. A terrible joke, but I do highly recommend you grab Vance's awesome book *Systematic Magic.*

Vance did a teleclass with my Pet Business Inner Circle members, and on that call he shared an exercise everyone can do to inject some 'WOW' into the customer service experience they offer.

He suggested you flow-chart your process for how someone comes into your business and what happens once they become a client.

- So, what happens when they land on your website?
- What happens when they fill in an application form?
- What happens when you answer the phone?
- What happens when they pay you a deposit?
- What happens when you meet them in person?
- What happens when they first sample your service?
- What happens when they refer someone?
- What happens when they give a testimonial?

Then once you've flow-charted it, you need to ask yourself, ' *How can I sprinkle some pixie dust on this process to create a 'WOW' experience?'*

This is very similar to the process I go through with my Private Pet Business Coaching Clients. We map out the customer journey and look for ways we can move people faster from being a warm lead to a paying customer, or from a semi-regular customer to someone who buys every day, or how can we move them from being a customer who buys your regular service to being a Premium 'Gold Service' Customer?

You can make a lot more money in your business by paying more attention to your business processes, and this is a great place to start.

Vance shared a great example of how he has Disnified the experience for the clients in his carpet cleaning business. The guys who work for him have a very special (and strict) process they follow which creates a unique and unforgettable experience.

- First up, when any of his guys attend an appointment, they park in the street, ***not*** on the driveway, just in case they have an oil leak on the van (something else they would have to clean up!) That's amazing attention to detail, something else Vance learned from Disney.
- Then they leave the van wearing a crisp, clean uniform (they also carry an extra uniform in the van in case they get dirty on a previous job).
- They carry with them a special rug (not to be confused with a magic carpet – Vance lives in Maryland, not Disneyland!), their toolbox, and a special gift for the client from Vance.
- When they reach the door, they lay down their special rug, they knock on the door rather than ring the bell (because *'friends knock, salespeople ring'* I LOVE THAT).
- They take a step back because the last thing the owner wants is to see a six-foot strapping tradesman leering through the glass at them.

- The door opens and the guy says, *'Hi, my name is Stephen. I'm here to create your healthy home. May I come in?'*
- Then, *before* entering they make an exaggeration of wiping their feet on the mat – remember they are performing a show here – and then when invited they enter the home and present the client with a gift.

Let me ask you, when was the last time you received a gift from a business you spent some money with?

Exactly!

It almost never happens.

The gift is just one part of a highly choreographed performance, with a tightly honed script to boot, and that is just the process for how they enter the home.

Imagine what kind of a performance they put on when they are assessing and cleaning the carpets.

Talk about WOW Factor!

And this is something you can do in your pet business.

Here are a few examples of how pet professionals can add 'WOW' to the everyday boring and mundane processes in their business.

These examples can be mixed and matched between professions, and they range from easy and inexpensive additions, to projects that require a little more work, but add a lot more WOW.

Dog walkers – Show the clients how safe their dogs are on your adventures by sharing videos that demonstrate your excellent control. And provide a quick and easy (and free) training programme for the client. After 10 walks, present your clients with a 'Canine Certificate of Adventurely Achievement' that tells them their dog is an official Member of the Pack. Once a quarter, hold an 'Open Day' for your pet parents to show them what you get up to on your adventures, and each client can (or must) bring one dog-owning friend to the 'show'.

Dog groomers – Reassure your new clients by creating a grooming system pictorial chart that shows them how you'll create the perfect experience for their dog. Take it a step further and make it a bespoke styling experience by letting the client choose which shampoo you use. Create a fake/pretend 'Grooming Magazine' that features your best clients' dogs as 'Canine Cover' girls (and boys).

Dog trainers – Provide a personalised video/tip sheet after every class/session that recaps key learning points and walks through next steps they need to take. At the end of your six weeks of puppy training, have a Canine Graduation where the puppies dash (or recall) to the front of the room to collect their graduation certificates, dressed up in puppy gowns and mortarboards.

Doggy Day care – Provide weekly 'school reports' for the dogs in your care. Invest in a school uniform type 'members only' apparel for dogs and their owners e.g. T-shirts, bandanas. Give recognition to your best clients by creating a 'Head Hound' of the week (like a head boy/girl) and profile their personality on your K9 Wall of Fame.

The basic premise is to think about how you can take an existing experience and 'plus' it.

So, if you currently give a packet of dog treats with a welcome pack, why not provide a personalised doggy cupcake, and cookie for the client as well.

Does this cost more?

Yes.

However, does it also enable you to charge more for the 'experience'?

Hell, yes!

And you don't need to spend BIG to create an awesome experience for your clients.

Remember, to surprise them, we need to give them something they *aren't* expecting, and something they generally wouldn't get from a 'regular' dog trainer/groomer/walker/day care.

There's loads you can do that's FREE, or certainly incredibly cheap.

When a new member joins the Pet Business Inner Circle, I send them a personalised video message to welcome them on board, and map out what is going to happen over the first few days and weeks as a PBIC member.

This costs nothing, except two minutes of my time.

Guess what, though…people appreciate that I took time to do that. I know because they message me all the time and tell me they appreciate it.

It *personalises* the experience.

It reassures them they've come to the right place to learn how to transform their pet business.

It shows them the face behind the business.

It also takes me just two minutes!

Seriously, if you haven't got a two-minute window in your daily routine to welcome aboard a brand-new PAYING client, then you need to seriously loosen up your schedule…

You've heard the expression 'First impressions last', right?

Well, this is your chance to make an unforgettable first impression, and seal the deal.

See, just because someone has invested in your pet service, that DOESN'T mean they are totally 100% happy.

There's such a thing as 'buyer's remorse'.

This is where someone buys something, but then they immediately regret it and want to cancel and get a refund.

Hopefully, your clients will put more time and effort into investing in a pet care service than they would from buying the latest gadget from Amazon…but this *doesn't* mean you can ignore the 'aftersales' part of the customer journey.

And you need to have a process in place that welcomes them to your business, and reassures them about the great service they are going to get from you.

As you'll find out later, the moment someone has invested in your services is actually the perfect time to upsell them, or sell them more of the service they've just bought.

So, make *'Send a personalised thank you video'* item number one on your to-do list.

The Power of Paper and Ink

If you've been to an event of mine, or invested in a programme, then as well as a personalised video you'll also have received a handwritten (or if I'm honest, badly scrawled) note or postcard.

A postcard, a second-class stamp and an envelope works out at about £1 each, every time I send one.

Can you really not afford to spend £1 to welcome a new client on board?

If not, you need to up your prices OR decide if running a business is really for you.

The Cost of Doing Business

Let's delve deeper into costs for a moment – or more specifically, customer appreciation costs.

When I talk about paper and ink marketing, and creating onboarding materials, I get a lot of people –usually freebie seekers who charge rock-bottom prices – asking me questions like:

'Do I really have to get the card printed, or can I send an e-card instead?'

To which my answer is, *'Only if you want to be a total cheapskate and devalue the whole experience.'*

I heard a cool story about how Disney custodians paint the fences overnight in Main Street, USA.

They use a special fast-drying paint, and they check the weather reports so they paint the fence at the optimum time, so the fence is as white as possible when the guests arrive.

That's a Disney-level attention to detail.

Other theme parks might try to save money by only painting the fences when they started to look tatty. But not Disney.

Similarly, you can't afford to be a Scrooge McDuck about providing a great customer experience.

Remember, the idea is we surprise, astonish and 'WOW' the client with the experience.

You tell me, is there more 'WOW' factor if you drop the card off yourself, ***or*** if you handwrite out the envelope, stamp it and send it in the post?

The answer is…sending it in the post is more impressive, and here's why:

First up, if they get a letter in the post, delivered by the postman, they have no idea who it's from so there's **instant curiosity.**

These days people rarely get nice things in the post, EVER!

If it's a handwritten note in a nice coloured envelope (or a box) then they'll be mega intrigued by what's inside, and it will jump straight to the top of the 'A' pile, i.e. the stuff that gets opened straight away.

THEN when they open it, they'll be surprised, delighted and hugely impressed you took the time and effort to think of them and send them a 'personal' message.

You've turned the whole 'sending a message' thang into a multi-step, emotional 'experience'.

Compare that to just leaving the card in their kitchen when you drop the dog off. It's still going to be appreciated, but it lacks the curiosity and surprise elements of receiving something in the post.

So, don't be cheap – and when you can, always try to 'plus' the experience to add more WOW Factor.

If you bought a copy of this book directly from me then you'll know exactly what I mean by a 'WOW Factor' package.

You thought you were getting a book, but you got a whole lot more.

I send out a bookmark, a chocolate bar, a CD, a newsletter, a thank you note and a voucher for a discount on more books, or one of my pet business programmes. (Incidentally, if you bought the eBook or audio version and you want the full paper and ink experience, go to www.petbusinessmarketing.com/magicbook).

So, why do I do this?

Because I know it works.

See, unlike most social-media-obsessed pet business gooroos, I teach AND I practise every kind of marketing, across all kinds of media, online AND offline.

You need to follow a similar approach.

Once you've started your 'WOW' process then you need to be consistent, and keep it up forever.

Every year I write around 300 personal postcards, make 200 personal videos for clients and prospects, as well as sending various other items throughout the year to my *Diamond, Platinum and Elite Mastermind* clients.

This cements the relationship I have with them AND – to come full circle – it adds to the stories they are telling about me.

Eventually, exceeding your client's expectations will become the norm, which should – nay, will – force you to up your game even more.

This is another factor that makes your business unique and 'uncopiable' by your competition.

By the time your competitors find out about the videos you send to new clients, you'll have added to the process, or 'plussed' it some other way.

At Disney, exceeding guests' expectations is the standard call of duty. It occurs at the end of a late-night shopping trip when the cashier takes the time to find out who you are and where you are staying, and then recommends the free boat ride back to your hotel and offers a map to the dock.

It's the plethora of these little wows, many of which seem fairly insignificant at the time, on which quality service depends.

If the little wows are delivered consistently and continuously, they add up to a big WOW.

In the next chapter, we're continuing the Disney journey as I show you how to add some punch and pixie dust to your pet business prices and promotions.

The Magic Kingdom marketers are experts at separating people from their cash, and making them feel good about doing so.

For now, I'd recommend you get stuck into 'plussing' your customer service experience.

Your existing customers are the bedrock of your business, and by plussing the experience you'll turn them into raving fans who can't stop telling their dog-owning friends about your amazing Doggy 'Disney' experience.

How you wow your clients this week will impact the stories they are telling about your business next week, next month, next year!

This applies whether you have one, two, ten or a hundred customers.

Make it memorable for them, and they'll tell people about it.

As your business grows and profitability increases, you can (and you should) invest more in making it an even better experience.

A final thought

Everything we cover in this book is outside of the box thinking, and you'll struggle to find anyone else in the pet industry talking about this kind of marketing, in this level of detail.

Social media hasn't had one mention, yet *that* is where 99% of the skint, pissed-off pet professionals will spend most of their time.

The social media loving guru's will roll their eyes or mock you if you suggest posting a personalised card to a new client.

Walt Disney experienced this. His own brother Roy distanced himself from the Disneyland idea which he thought was crazy. He said it was too expensive, too risky, and refused to fund the idea until Walt got TV companies involved in financing.

If you want to be successful in life and business then you need to be prepared to go against the grain.

Embrace the ideas I've shared with you here, and THEN take action!

Chapter Summary

- **Map Out a Customer Journey –** Make a list of all the processes and activities that happen in your business each day, and start sprinkling pixie dust on each individual activity. To stimulate word of mouth you should start with all the customer-facing processes. Take inspiration from great customer service moments you've experienced and modify them for your business.

- **Have Fun!** – There are times to be serious in business, but this is a time to release your inner child and have some serious fun. Push yourself out of your comfort zone, and don't wimp out because you think your clients are too sophisticated. They aren't! And they will love the fact that you are investing time and effort in creating a wow experience for them and their dogs.

- **Be Memorable** – This doesn't mean spending lots of money, although you should have a customer appreciation budget built into your outgoings. Start small with handwritten notes and personalised communications. Go the extra mile to surprise your clients, and you'll have them telling stories and raving about your wonderful way of doing business.

BONUS TRAINING – Paper-and-ink swipe file. I've put together a swipe file of great paper-and-ink marketing materials I've collected over the years. These are real-life examples of how companies in different industries have used paper and ink to improve and enhance the customer experience. There are 25 videos in total, and you can see all of them by going to www.petbusinessmarketing.com/magicgift

Chapter Two

Why Your Hero Pet Business Needs a Vicious Villain

'You poor, simple fools. Thinking you could defeat me. Me! The mistress of all evil!'

Maleficent

If I asked you to name the baddest Disney villain, who would you choose?

Murderous Maleficent from *Sleeping Beauty*?

Power-hungry Scar from *The Lion King*?

Dog thief Cruella de Vil?

My own personal favourite is probably Madame Medusa from *The Rescuers.*

Medusa is the proprietor of a seedy pawn shop in New York City. She is greedy, obsessed with diamonds and has two pet crocodiles named Brutus and Nero.

Come on, what's not to like?

Her desire for diamonds consumes Medusa to the extent that she is prepared to kidnap the orphan Penny and take her to the Devil's Bayou, where she places her in a bucket, lowers her into a cave at low tide and doesn't let her out until she finds The Devil's Eye, the world's biggest Diamond.

Medusa means business, and poor Penny almost drowns as a result.

It's interesting that although Disney films are aimed at little children, they sure are packed with horror, evil, treachery, betrayal and even death.

Look at the list of crimes committed by your favourite Disney baddies:

Gaston from *Beauty and the Beast* – attempted murder, kidnapping, breaking and entering, assault and battery, arson, incitement to riot.

Or the Evil Queen from *Snow White* – attempted murder, conspiracy to commit murder, criminal witchcraft, poisoning, negligence, fraud, resisting arrest, tyranny. (To be fair to her, with a name like 'Evil Queen' we shouldn't have expected much else.)

Or what about Captain Hook from *Peter Pan*, who these days would be charged with piracy, murder, attempted murder, kidnapping and terroristic threats?

Quite the rap sheet, I'm sure you'll agree.

But there's a very good reason these gruesome guys and gals are pure devils.

In any kind of storytelling, the villain is just as important as the good guy. In fact, in many ways the villain is *more* important.

Think about it: would you have cared as much for Luke Skywalker if Darth Vader wasn't his dad?

Would *Die Hard* be the Christmas classic it has become (and for the record, *Die Hard* IS a Christmas movie) without the calculating Hans Gruber?

This doesn't just apply to movies. Who would Doctor Who be without the Daleks, or He-Man without Skeletor, or Buffy the Vampire Slayer without Spike?

Even in professional wrestling, every major superstar good guy needs a similarly major badass enemy, or 'heel' as it's known in the trade.

The same applies when you are marketing your pet services.

You need a villain of the piece.

You need to identify some terrible outcome that dog owners in your town are suffering from that only *your* service can thwart.

And in your marketing, you need to highlight this huge agony-inflicting ache that keeps your prospects awake at night, and position your superpower as the solution.

Most pet business owners <u>never</u> think about this.

They only talk about the positive aspects, attributes and outcomes of their service.

So, your standard pet professional will have a website and advertising materials that read something like this:

Come to our day care, we love dogs!

Or

Let me groom your dog, he will look lovely afterwards!

Or

I walk dogs. Please let me walk yours!

Any of that sound familiar?

Now, if you were running a pet business 30 or 40 years ago when there were hardly any day cares, trainers, walkers or groomers around, then that kind of advertising might be OK.

If someone needs a doggy day care and you are the only choice in your town, then it's fine to have an advertisement that says 'We are a doggy day care'.

Nowadays though, competition for your services is everywhere. There's been a proliferation of pet businesses in every town and city in the Western world.

If you are lucky enough to have little, or zero, competition in your location, then enjoy it while it lasts because trust me, competition ***is*** coming to a town near you.

Part of the reason is most pet professions have a very low barrier to entry, and you can start a dog day care or dog walking business with no previous experience at all. Even dog training or grooming skills can be learned in a fairly short space of time.

This means there are lots of people out there who hate their jobs and love dogs, who are prepared to have a go at running a pet business in your town.

The pandemic has accelerated this process. Unsurprisingly, many people who were furloughed or forced to work from home really enjoyed it and started to think about changing jobs. A new career in the pet service sector provided an easy escape route for them.

This means there are more and more pet businesses competing for work, AND it's only going to get worse.

Now, you can hide under the bed and ignore the problem, OR you can do something about it.

One way to protect your pet business, or supercharge the growth of a new business, is to master how to market your services.

Marketing by only talking about the positive elements of your service WON'T make you stand out, OR help you connect with distressed dog owners in your town.

Why?

Because that's what everyone else does!

You need to put your prospect's pain points, or the 'villain' of the piece, front and centre with your marketing.

Your marketing simply won't work as well without a villain.

Just like Disney movies wouldn't work without a villain.

Without a villain, the story of *Beauty and the Beast* would read: *Avid reader from French village meets grumpy outcast and falls in love.*

Without a villain, *The Jungle Book* would read: *Lost boy lives happily ever after in jungle with animal friends.*

Without a villain, *Bambi* would just be: *Mother deer and her fawn eat grass in a forest.*

Which would be incredibly boring, right?

Well, that's what your advertisements look like without a villain.

Now, here's the thing:

Your villain is not necessarily a person. It's more of a feeling.

- A worry
- A fear
- An anxiety
- A danger
- A frustration
- A pain point

It's something that causes your potential client unpleasantness, distress and even causes them to wake up in the middle of the night in a panic-induced cold sweat, too anxious to go back to sleep.

Goodness, this Disnify your pet business thang has taken a dark turn, has it not…?

Please don't think these fears and frustrations don't exist.

They most definitely do.

Dog owners who have jobs feel guilty about leaving their dogs home alone. They leave the television on, spend any amount of money on fluffy toys for the dogs to play with, and then can't concentrate when they are at work because they are worried about the dog.

Reactive dog owners not only suffer from the actual pain of walking their dogs who pull, lunge and bark at other dogs, but they also experience incredible frustration and embarrassment. They dread the time when the clock strikes 'walkies!'

Puppy owners worry about their new puppy destroying their house, biting their children and they are terrified that the puppy will grow up to be a naughty dog or even a dangerous dog.

Owners of nervous and anxious dogs hate taking them to the groomers because they know the dog will get stressed out. A stressed dog = a stressed owner who feels like a 'bad' dog mum/dad.

Those are the pain points you need to talk about when you are promoting your services.

Many pet business owners are shrinking violets who shy away from even trying this.

They think it seedy and immoral to talk about the prospect's pain.

But if you truly care about helping people with your service then you will ignore these sensitive snowflakes and get serious about addressing the issues they care most deeply about.

In your town there are hundreds if not thousands of distressed dog owners suffering from all kinds of problems that they would happily pay money to have a professional take care of…so why isn't your phone ringing off the hook?

Part of it is down to a lack of awareness that your service exists, and the other part is a lack of trust in your ability to help them.

We can resolve the lack of trust and awareness by sharing our story, our signature system and testimonials, but we need something more than that to get their attention in the first place, and we do that by talking about their main pain point in all our marketing materials.

Starting with the pain point has three BIG advantages:

1. First up is **attention**. Just like when training a dog, the first thing you need is attention, and

using pain points gets attention. Problems have always been a big deal for us humans and we notice the problems. Ugg the caveman used to be wary when he heard a rustling in the bushes, because that could have represented a life-threatening problem, like a sabre-toothed tiger who wanted to eat him. Dog owners in your town have problems too, and you'll get their attention by talking about them in your marketing.

2. The second advantage to leading with pain points in your advertising is that it creates an immediate level of **trust** between you and the prospect. It doesn't mean they will necessarily buy your service straight away, but they will be more inclined to read the rest of the advert, and copy down your contact details, because you are showing you understand the problems they are suffering from. This is very different to the kind of adverts your competition are doing. Consequently, it'll make your adverts stand out.

3. The third is **urgency**. With any kind of advert we put out there, we want the reader to take some kind of action. Either to move towards investing in our services, or if not, then to certainly move closer towards buying. Well, when we use pain points, we remind the dog owner of the problem that is causing them a lot of stress, anxiety, and worry. Then, if you can position your service as the antidote to the poison, you'll cause the prospect to take action faster.

The solution – your service – is more attractive when we put the problem – the pain the dog owner is suffering from – front and centre.

Framing your prospects' BIG problem as the 'villain' and your amazing service as the 'hero' will transform how effective your pet business adverts are.

Here's a simple V - S - H *(Villain – Suffering – Hero)* formula you can use to help you punch up your marketing materials, so they speak to the kind of clients you are looking for.

We start with 'V' which is the villain of the piece.

The villain represents the bad outcome the dog owner is suffering from.

If you're a dog trainer, the villain might be the distraction that causes an owner's dog to run away from them in the park.

If you're a day care owner, the villain might be the boredom and lack of exercise that causes the sad, stuck-at-home dog to howl and chew the furniture.

If you're a dog groomer, the villain might be the worry the owner experiences because they don't know how their dog is being treated at the grooming salon.

The villain is the big challenge or problem that consumes your potential client. It brings them endless worry, stress and frustration. It spoils their dog-owning experience and makes them wish upon a star they could fix it.

The 'S' in the formula stands for Suffering. This is the pain the villain causes the dog owner. If the villain is what the problem is, then the suffering is – as the name suggests – how it makes them feel.

The suffering could be the fear a dog owner feels when the dog doesn't recall and takes off into the woods.

It could be the embarrassment they experience when their dog barks and lunges at another dog on a walk.

It could be the guilt that consumes them every time they leave the dog home alone.

Finally, there's the Hero, which, it shouldn't surprise you to learn, is your service – the solution to their problem.

You need to pitch your pet service as the answer to all their prayers.

If you structure your copy in the way I describe, the reader will be eager to urgently contact you to help them out.

Here's an example of how I used the V-S-H formula in an advert for my *How to Be Your Dog's Superhero* book:

Do you love your dog but wish he would listen to you, and are your daily-walks stress-filled affairs? *That's your* ***villain.***

Does the thought of letting your dog off lead give you a panic attack? *There's your* ***suffering.***

Then you need to grab your copy of *How To Be Your Dog's Superhero: Transform Your Dastardly Dog Using The Power Of Play . And my book is the* ***'hero'.***

You should do this on all your promotional material.

Everything from your website, to your leaflets, postcards, newsletters, blog articles and social media posts.

Remember, if you're struggling to get interest in your 'hero' service, it's probably because you haven't done a good enough job describing the 'villain'!

Chapter Summary

Track Down Your Villain – A hero is only as good as the villain, so spend time identifying what is your ideal client's BIG worry/frustration/fear/problem. You can do this by talking to your existing clients about what challenges they faced before they started working with you. Ask questions, go deep, take lots of notes, and you'll have a lot of material to use in your copy.

Pain Points = Profits – Us humans are attracted to pain points. Often, we are more motivated to make decisions that move us away from painful outcomes than we are to move towards a pleasurable one. Don't think this is too much of a 'salesy' way for you to sell. If you embrace this you'll attract more of the dog owners you want to work with, which means you can help more people with your services.

Zero to Hero – You know as well as I do that your service can change the lives of dog owners in your town, but you won't get their attention talking about all the benefits without first highlighting the villain. Humans are attracted to problems, and you'll get more attention on your adverts by introducing the bad guy first, so use the V-S-H formula to maximise sales.

BONUS TRAINING: To help you better tap into your ideal client's fears, frustrations and failures, I am giving you FREE access to a special 60-minute audio training that I've only previously shared with my *Diamond* private coaching clients – In ***Seven Psychological Sales Triggers*** you'll discover how to easily connect with more dog owners about their pooch problems. This will transform the effectiveness of your website copy, social media posts and any other articles and sales pieces you produce. To claim this FREE resource now, go to: www.petbusinessmarketing.com/magicgift

Chapter Three

How to Prince Charm Your Pet Business Prices!

'You don't have time to be timid. You must be bold and daring!'

Lumiere

My wife Beth and I took the kids to Disneyland Paris in 2008 and again in 2011.

We stayed onsite at the Explorers Hotel, which was pretty basic and a bit of a bun fight at mealtimes, but overall, very clean and tidy.

Toby was three years old and Alex was ten, and because of the age difference we spent most of the mornings together, but in the afternoon we would split up for a couple of hours. So Beth would take Toby to do some of the kiddies' rides and shows, and Alex and I would indulge in the big boy rollercoasters.

The big lads headed off to Thunder Mountain while Beth and Toby checked out Buzz Lightyear's Laser Blast. As the name suggests, this is a shoot-em-up ride where you have to blast as many aliens as you can to get the highest score possible.

Toby loved the ride, so much so that all four of us went back later to experience it together.

On the way out of the initial ride, as Beth was popping him back in his pushchair, little three-year-old Toby said, *'I think I'll have a Buzz Lightyear now, Mammy.'*

Now, we spoil our kids as much as anyone else, so obviously Toby got his Buzz Lightyear…suckers!

And if you've tried something new and had a great experience, then buying something that allows you to remember the experience is the next logical step, right?

Well, it is at Disney.

After every single ride you have to make your way through a gift shop that is jam-packed with high-end memorabilia to tempt you to part you with your pounds, dollars and sheckles.

All the gift shops are themed individually so they are aligned perfectly with the ride you've just been on.

So, when you exit Star Tours, or Pirates of the Caribbean, and you're feeling pumped from the experience, you then get the chance to build a lightsaber, or buy a pirate hat (or in our case, a Buzz Lightyear toy).

I call this ***seamless sequential selling,*** and it's something any pet business owner can do.

To make this happen you don't need a pop-up souvenir stall to appear whenever someone buys something from you, but you can ensure that every time you sell one of your services, it leads seamlessly on to the sale of another, complementary service.

That second part is key.

Did you know the number one time to sell to a customer is immediately after they've bought something from you?

Well, it is!

Let's go back to the customer journey at Disney for a second.

Most people, like me, Beth and the kids, have saved up, bought tickets, booked flights, dreamed about and looked forward to going to Disney for a *long time.*

And once you finally arrive you are naturally in a happy 'buying' frame of mind.

You're also captive inside a closed environment where there's nothing to do but have fun (and spend more money).

This is almost exactly the same as the customer journey your clients go on.

See, it can take a long time to get a prospect warm enough to buy from you. Sometimes it happens fast, over a couple of days, but often it can take weeks, month and even years.

That's because some people are in desperate need of your service NOW, whereas most prospects are casually looking at your service from afar, or they are happy with their current provider and haven't noticed your business yet.

Eventually they'll pick up a leaflet, see your branded van about town, spot an advertisement in a local paper, or they'll see your social media content and finally stumble onto your website.

All the heavy lifting is done BEFORE they buy, with the educational and entertaining marketing and follow-up you have in place.

Hopefully, you've used the Villains, Suffering, Hero formula to push their buttons, agitated all their pain points and convinced them you are the best, most trusted pet professional, which means you're the only expert option they are considering contacting.

By then they've probably read testimonials, heard friends refer you, read stories about your 'Disney-like' levels of service and even dreamed about the amazing 'results' they are going to get when they hire you.

All this means that when they are ready to commit to a purchase, and they flip from prospect to customer, they are literally at 'boiling point'.

Which also means if you offer them more services (and products) while they are still 'on the boil', many will buy more from you, as sure as night follows day.

This is where upsells and cross-sells come into play.

Let's define these strategies:

Upsell: An upsell is when you offer the customer a larger quantity of something they've agreed to buy, OR an upgraded or premium version of the same thing. For example, a full day care session instead of a half-day session.

Cross-sell: A cross-sell is when you offer a related item. For example, a dog walker might offer home boarding services, or a dog groomer might also offer their clients treats or some doggy apparel in a shop in the salon.

Upsells, and selling higher-priced services, are where the easy money is to be made.

If you're an inexperienced pet business owner, or you aren't too savvy about business and marketing, then you might be thinking, *'Why do I need to offer something at a higher price than my regular service?'*

And the honest answer is, you don't.

If you want you can just sell one standard price service to all your customers, forever. However, if you do that then you are potentially leaving a LOT of money on the table.

See, there are three ways you can make more money in your business. They are:

1. Increase your prices
2. Sell more stuff to your existing clients
3. Sell to more clients

Once you start implementing the marketing secrets I've shared with you in this book then your reputation will increase and you'll be able to increase your prices more easily. You'll certainly be able to charge vastly more than your average competitors.

Most pet business owners ignore upsells, shy away from price increases and only ever concentrate on option number three, which is to sell to more clients.

Now, to a degree we all need to have new clients regularly coming through the door. If you are a new business then acquiring new clients is your main priority, and even if you are full then you should be putting people on a waiting list.

However, it won't take too long for you to fill your diary, and pretty soon you'll have no more space for new clients, so what do you do then if you want to earn more money?

The answer is to concentrate on the first two ways to grow your business which are:

1. Increase prices
2. Sell more stuff to your existing clients

You can even create a whole menu of amazing options with all kinds of added extras that your clients will LOVE buying from you.

See, it's far easier to sell more services to your existing clients than it is to find a completely new client.

As I mentioned earlier, you usually need to invest a lot of time, money and energy to get a new client. And you often need to wait a long time until they are ready to buy from you.

Selling to your existing clients is easier because they *already* know you, they've already used your service, and they're happy with what they are buying, which means they'll probably buy more from you, IF you offer it to them.

I'd go so far as to suggest your existing clients are sitting at home right now, stroking their dogs' ears and sniffing their paws thinking, *'What can I buy that will make you happier, my lovely doggy?'*

This means you should be offering your existing customers a range of services that ascend in price.

Some of your clients will skip past your low-priced offering and jump straight to your highest-priced service. Here's a little upsell story of my own to more easily make the point:

In 2017 we moved to our current house, an old farmhouse on the edge of Sunderland. It has a few rundown barns, and a big open enclosed garden that allowed us to realise our dream of owning chickens.

So, a few months after we moved in, off I went with Toby my youngest to a local hen and poultry supply centre.

We picked the hens we wanted and then headed to the store to get the supplies. Being inexperienced owners, we were advised what to get by the proprietor.

When it came to choosing the feeder, the chicken expert picked two plastic hoppers off the shelf and said this one is £9, or this one is a lot better for £14.

I barely heard her because I was transfixed on the stainless-steel hopper on the shelf behind her.

The one that I'd seen free range chickens feeding from on a hundred TV shows like *The Darling Buds of May.*

The one she hadn't even bothered showing me.

'Erm, I want that one,' I told her.

'OK, but that's a lot more expensive,' she said.

I didn't care about that, so I bought the hopper and a stainless-steel drinking trough to go with it.

Remember, getting chickens was for us one of our life goals at the time. This was something we'd dreamed about for years, and we weren't going to skimp on our dream.

Similarly, many of your clients care passionately about their dogs. They'll do anything, and spend anything, to make their dog happy, because if their dog is happy then *they* are happy.

Which means they'll gladly upgrade and invest in your higher-priced services.

Here are a few examples of some easy-peasy (and extremely profitable) upsells:

A dog groomer who sells a regular grooming session should have little trouble selling a higher-priced 'luxury' groom, where you add a blueberry facial, teeth cleaning and a goody bag to take home.

A dog walker should easily be able to tempt an owner who bought a regular walk with a more exclusive 'bells and whistles' training walk/adventure. Or if they've bought one session you should easily be able to get them to buy two or three sessions (thus doubling or tripling your fee).

A dog trainer who sells a puppy class should be able to upsell the owner to a one-to-one 'fast-track' session, or a 'next-level' follow-on class.

A lot of pet business owners cock up the upsell opportunity by offering the wrong kind of upsell.

So, they'll sell a groom/walk/training session but then instead of an all-singing and all-dancing version of the thing they've sold, they will instead offer a brush/treats/training lead as the upsell.

I'm not a huge fan of this because it's more of a cross-sell than an upsell, and I think the easier money comes from offering an enhanced version of the service they're already buying from you.

Also, you can generally only sell someone one lead/brush/harness, whereas you can sell them a recurring higher-priced service many times.

You need to put some thought into this, and if you don't have a range of services (that ascend in price) then putting that in place should be your first course of action.

The key principle is to offer at the time of sale, or shortly afterwards, an increased quantity or an upgraded version of the original service, or relevant additional items you think your clients will be interested in.

If your customer declines the upsell when you first offer it to them, then you can (and you should) offer the upsell again, and again, and again until they buy.

Obviously, you don't strong-arm them into buying more stuff and say, ' *Buy this amazing adventure, or else!'* Instead, you gently remind them of the other things you offer.

You should remind them using all kinds of media, especially paper and ink, and also use videos and testimonials from clients who already buy your higher-priced services.

Here's an example. Let's say I did a meet and greet with a client and they wanted to invest in a mini dog adventure.

If I thought the dog would benefit then I would immediately offer the full, higher-priced adventure.

By 'offer' I mean tell them about it and sell the benefits.

I wouldn't necessarily give a discount, although there's nothing wrong with doing a £5 off your first adventure promotion to get the client moving.

I'd get my diary out and say *'Hmmm, let me see, I can book his first mini adventure for Tuesday, and I'm actually a little quiet on Friday for the full adventure, so that would be a great time for Bonzo to come and experience a full adventure. Shall I book him in for that?'*

If they said no, then I reply, *'No problem. Assuming he enjoys his mini adventure we can get him in for a full adventure the following week, if you like?'*

Then I'd leave some kind of service menu that highlights all the benefits of the full adventure, that also includes a bunch of testimonials from happy clients, AND I may even send them a video of ***'What we get up to on a MEGA Pack Leader Dog Adventure'.***

Then I'd just keep offering the full adventure until they bought it.

The thing is, if you've thought out the offering (made it better, bigger, shinier, more luxurious and beneficial), and also remember to present it in an exciting way, then you won't need to sell the shit out of it.

People gladly invest in higher-priced services that bring them additional benefits.

My Pet Business Inner Circle is a great example of that.

There's the *PBIC Gold Level* which offers mainly information and the opportunity to ask questions via monthly Q & As, and in the Forum.

Then there's the *Diamond Private Coaching*, where you get more personal help from me to create a bespoke pet business plan, and small group accountability to help keep you on track.

Above that there is the *Platinum Private Coaching* which is for more established pet businesses who want to scale and develop further and move forward faster.

I also have an *Elite* Mastermind level added to the mix for people who have established six-figure and seven-figure pet businesses.

There's no real hard sell with any of these additional services. Yes, I tell them about it, but only because I know some people will make a lot more progress, a lot faster, if they upgrade.

The services I offer are designed to fit the needs of pet business owners who want more help and support, and who want to get results faster.

Similarly, your clients will need, want, and desire more in-depth and comprehensive services from you.

Someone who's buying a regular dog groom will benefit from having a super-duper luxury groom (as will the dog).

Someone who's buying a dog walk, training session or day care place will benefit from investing in a more comprehensive service that makes the dog happier and makes life easier for the client.

So, make sure you have these 'extras' on your service menu, and don't forget to offer them!

The key with upsells and cross-sells is to have a system in place that automatically offers the upsell to the client.

At Disney you'll get offered various upsells at each stage of your customer journey.

When you arrive, you'll be offered standard or preferred parking ($25 or $45 per day).

When you buy tickets at a Disney theme park if you ask for a seven-day ticket, you might be invited to consider a ten-day ticket instead, because the cost of adding three additional days is relatively small.

You might consider an add-on option that allows you to tag on a visit to a water park, or park hopper option (for an extra fee).

In the park, if you want to buy a drink, you'll have the option to 'upgrade' to a souvenir cup or mug, which are highly collectable for the customer – and highly profitable for Disney.

And before you even get on a plane you can plan your meals with a Disney meal plan upsell package, your photographs with a Memory Maker pass, and now you can even save time visiting each ride to book your Digital Premier Access Fast pass with a brand-new ($20 per person, per day) Maxpass option.

Then there are character meals, guided tours, and other exclusive offerings that cater to the needs of those who can afford them.

The upsells are never-ending, and people are happy to pay!

We ended up spending a fortune on top of everything we'd pre-paid for before we got there.

You can quickly identify some easy upsell opportunities by flow-charting your sales process.

This is something I do with all my private clients as it's a great way to sniff out the 'hidden money' in your business.

- What happens and what else gets offered when someone phones you up and books an appointment/session?
- What gets offered when someone buys something?
- What do you offer when you've delivered a service?
- What gets offered when they've bought the upsell? (Do you have another upsell they can buy? Because you'd better believe you need an offer in place for that too!)

We're going to finish this chapter by deep-diving on a Disney pricing strategy which perfectly demonstrates why price, and price alone, can make ALL the difference to your business success.

In the mid-eighties, attendance at the Disney parks limped along without any major increase in numbers, yet revenues soared…

Much of the growth of the whole Disney company had been nurtured through a very simple funding device: jacking up the prices at the gate.

Remember from earlier, increasing prices was number one on our three ways to grow your business, and as Disney found it was the easiest way to increase profits.

Ten price increases boosted the adult price at Disneyland to $21.50 by 1988.

Disney chiefs worked out that each $1 increase at the gate resulted in an extra $26 million added to the bottom line.

This backs up what I've always taught about pricing. Namely that it pays to be premium.

We've touched upon 'lifetime customer value' in this chapter, and this Disney price increase ratchet is a great example of how you seriously increase lifetime customer value, by increasing prices.

Every pound you increase your prices by will drive BIG BUCKS into your bottom line.

Imagine you have a dog walking client who uses you three times a week and stays for five years.

A £1 increase in prices nets you an extra £720

A £3 increase in prices nets you an extra £2,160

A £5 increase nets you an extra £3,600

A £10 increase nets you an extra £7,200

Let's say you have just 10 clients. That's an extra £72,000 in the next five years. JUST by increasing prices.

You didn't have to do any extra marketing, promoting or even get any extra clients to achieve that.

And that's just the start because those who spend more on a premium service are often willing to invest even more over time.

This is called the multiplier effect

Disney marketing studies had picked up on this peculiar phenomenon: the more people spend at the gate, the more they spend inside the park.

The new attractions convinced people to stay longer, eat more, and spend more in the shops and hotels.

And, while the promotions encouraged people to come to the parks, the higher prices discouraged the less affluent.

By 1990, the median household income of the households coming through those gates had reached $44,500, 38 percent above the national average.

This means by aggressively increasing prices Disney attracted more affluent clients.

I've noticed this in my dog adventure business.

Every time I increase prices our best clients use us more often.

One of my *Elite* members, Tim Jackson, noticed this same phenomenon when we introduced a membership into his day care operation. Yes, you read that right. His clients have to be paying monthly members just to use his day care facility.

And YES, by committing to being 'the premium exclusive service provider' in your town you are going to target your services at those who can afford them (and disqualify those who can't afford your high prices).

That comes with the turf I'm afraid.

You can't have one without the other, but I'm sure in time you'll get over the hardship of not dealing with chav clients who complain about your prices and pay late, if it means you make more money with less stress and fewer headaches.

Disney took this premium pricing one step further and in 1987 they created their own currency, Disney Dollars! These came in $1, $5 and $10 bills.

When you bought something at a Disney Park, you could take your change either in regular currency, or in 'Disney Dollars,' which could only be spent on Disney property. Surprisingly, people loved this funny money. In fact, most of it was never redeemed — it found its way home as another souvenir.

Genius!

Could you do something similar in your business?

Yes.

More importantly, is this something your competition would do?

Noooooo.

Disney didn't get where they are by copying the competition. You won't either.

Be bold with your ideas.

Think BIG with your plans.

Be premium with your pricing.

Add to what you already offer to maximise profits.

Chapter Summary

When putting together your upsell, think 'Creativity' and 'Customer'.

How can you wow the client and create a whizzbang offer that trounces the competition?

You do that by putting the customer first, listening to their feedback and thinking about what THEY want.

What is going to make them AND their dog happy. Or happier!

Start there and you won't go far wrong.

We all LOVE upsells – Sometimes pet business owners will tell me, '*My clients don't want upsells.*' They are usually the same pet business owners who are skint, tired and pissed off at their lack of income. There might be a small percentage of people who don't buy upsells, but most of us do. Affluent clients are used to buying upsells and will seek out the higher-priced option, so without an upsell in place you are stopping them spending more money with you.

Win-win for upsell success – The way to ensure your upsells are exciting and enticing for your clients is to make sure they – and their dog – are benefitting. If you put the client's needs first then they'll invest in your upsells, eventually. Put your Walt hat on and think, 'How can I "plus" this groom/walk/training or day care session?' and remember to charge for the extra experience.

To make more, charge more – I've seen the multiplier effect work in hundreds of my private clients' businesses. When you charge higher prices then you'll attract more of the clients who can afford your higher prices, who are the kind of people who buy upsells, which means you'll make vastly more profit overall.

BONUS TRAINING : To help you effortlessly add more value to your pet business without even taking on a single new client, I'm giving you FREE access to my ***Unbelievable Pet Business Upsells Masterclass***. In this exclusive training I'll show you how to effortlessly add higher-priced services to your existing service menu. You'll be able to plug these upsell ideas straight into your service offering so you can make more money from your existing clients. To claim this FREE resource now, go to www.petbusinessmarketing.com/magicgift

Chapter Four

Storyselling Your 5-Star Service

'All it takes is faith and trust... Oh! And something I forgot: Dust. Just a little bit of pixie dust.'

Peter Pan

One of my favourite Disney movies growing up was *Basil the Great Mouse Detective.*

You may not have heard of it, but I have fond memories of watching this in my primary school hall. You know, those special no-work, non-uniform days when you could bring a toy in…ah, happy days.

Originally called *Basil of Baker Street,* there was a bit of a fiasco before the film was released, when the Disney marketing department decided the name was 'too British' and asked the animators to suggest new titles.

In the end, all the animators' suggestions were ignored, and the marketing department renamed it *The Great Mouse Detective.*

This incensed the Disney animators who lampooned what they considered the unimaginative, generic sound of the new name in a fake memo that 'announced' that all Disney classics would be renamed — this memo that showed up in the *Los Angeles Times.*

The new names included *Seven Little Men Help a Girl* (for *Snow White and the Seven Dwarfs*), *Color and Music* (for *Fantasia*), *The Girl with the See-Through Shoes* (for *Cinderella)* and *A Boy, a Bear and a Big Black Cat* (for *The Jungle Book*).

Just like in the movies, business and brand names are crucial to the success of a venture.

What you name your pet business – and your individual services – will massively affect how easy it is for new customers to find you and what their first impression is of your business. Sadly, most pet businesses put little thought into the name that communicates their business identity.

A lot of business owners are tempted to play it safe, but if you give your pet business a boring name that is very similar to what your competition are called, then you make it incredibly hard to stand out.

Essentially, you handicap yourself before you've even started doing any marketing.

So, in this chapter we're going to deep-dive into how you can get creative with how you present your services, so you can more easily stand out from the competition, and attract the right kind of client.

And creativity is something that Disney is famous for, through their Imagineering process...

Imagineering is a portmanteau formed from imagination and engineering, but contrary to Disney mythology, Walt Disney *didn't* actually create the word. Imagineering was used by Alcoa in the 1940s in their advertising to promote what they considered to be imaginative approaches to engineering.

Creativity can come into play whenever you have the opportunity to generate new ideas, solutions or approaches.

And in your role as the marketer of your pet business, you have lots of these opportunities.

Blending creative know-how and technical knowledge can apply to any sort of task.

A bin lorry driver who devises a new collection route can be thought to have 'imagineered the new collection system'.

A chef who combines spices and herbs in a unique way can be thought of as a 'culinary imagineer'.

A dog trainer who creates an Olympics-themed training session can be said to have 'imagineered' a new lesson.

Disney Imagineers have a set of principles they use to help them come up with the most imaginative ideas possible, and to help stimulate your mind and get your creative juices flowing we'll cover three of them now.

Imagineering Principle One – it all starts with a story

I had an interesting call with one of my *Elite Mastermind* members Tony 'Magic Hands' Sherry recently.

During his last 90-day goals call we identified that he needs to 'sell more' to existing clients. The 'something else' needs to be a natural upsell to his existing services, and ideally – as with any upsell – it should be something the client will gladly pay for, but which won't add substantially to Tony's workload.

After a bit of to-ing and fro-ing, we came up with a meditation upsell. This gives the client a method for relaxing with their dog – which is very useful, or you could argue is essential after they've just taken part in one of Tony's therapy sessions.

Tony quickly came up with three cool meditations and sold them the next week.

A great example of the 'fast-action taking' and 'outside the box' thinking you can only get from my private coaching; however, that's not the point of this story.

See, Tony informed me that for the meditations to be effective they need to take the listener on a journey. An immersive, emotive experience with sights, smells and other sensory descriptions that make the journey feel authentic.

As he was describing the process I was immediately transported to my favourite dog walk – which, seeing as you asked, is a meander along the river at Reeth in the heart of the Yorkshire Dales – but before I got the chance to finish my daydream (and the pint of make believe Black Sheep I was supping in the pub after the walk), I interrupted Tony by blurting out *'That's exactly what Disney does!'*

Storytelling is something that Disney are absolute masters of, and Imagineers have played a key role in the Disney organisation's successful storytelling since the 1940s.

Stories and characters are so important that in 2006 Disney chief Bob Iger started a 'character and talent acquisition' programme that saw Disney spend over $15 billion on Pixar, Star Wars and Marvel.

However, storytelling at Disney goes beyond the exploits of Iron Man, Buzz Lightyear and R2-D2…

Storytelling runs through the whole organisation.

Just like Walt before him, another former Disney CEO, Michael Eisner, looked on the theme parks as an extension of his sense of story:

'It's basically the same business. An attraction in one of our parks is like a film, in that it has to have a theme and tell a story. And I know a good story always has a beginning, middle, and end.'

He applied this point of view not only to the attractions, but to the parks themselves, the hotels in them, even the restaurants and stores.

He said: 'We ask, *"What is the story we want to tell when people walk into one of our new buildings? What are they going to feel? What is going to happen next? And how will it end?"'*

I get my private clients to storyboard their customers' journey this way, and you'd benefit also from mapping out what you want your customer experience to look like, from start to finish.

One of the reasons Disney excels with their parks and hotels is because of another principle Imagineers call Blue Sky Speculation.

Imagineering Principle Two – Blue Sky Speculation

Blue Sky Speculation means that any idea must be presented in the boldest way possible without considering any potential limitations.

Imagineers live by the slogan, *'If you can dream it, you can do it.'* And for them there's no such thing as impossible; if the idea is good enough, they'll figure out a way to make it happen.

I get my students to do a similar exercise at my Pet Business Bootcamps. I split the attendees up into groups, and they brainstorm lots of ideas until they've come up with the ultimate version of their service.

I say, *'Imagine if money was no object; what would the Ultimate Dog Walk/dog groom/training/doggy day care session look like?'*

Now, not all the ideas are going to be practical or immediately implementable, but they will all have merit, and they'll force you to think a bit bigger and aim your sights a bit higher.

And ideas are what we want.

Imagineers never kill a good idea. If it can't be done right now or won't fit within the parameters of logistics, they are known to put a pin in an idea and return to it later – sometimes years or even decades later.

Sometimes the ideas appear as they were envisioned, and other times they appear in a totally different form.

Storytelling is key to the success of your business, and there are three main types of stories you can tell in your marketing:

1. **Your origin story** – This can be your personal and business story. When you tell your origin story, you are communicating WHY you do what you do. Yes, you are selling a service, but people buy people, and you'll connect with more dog owners and convince them that you can be trusted if you tell your doggy origin story.

2. **Behind-the-scenes stories** – Rather than talking about how you can help dog owners, you can give them a peek behind the curtain by showing them exactly what you are up to. You can write articles, do videos and write emails where you demonstrate a training/walking/grooming/day care issue that you've dealt with that day.

3. **The story of your client's journey** – This can be anything from a simple story to a more complex case study, but it's told through the eyes of your client and the experience they had. These testimonial-type stories are very powerful because rather than you talking about your results, someone else is recommending you, so it's more believable.

Next up we have the principle of creative intent.

Imagineering Principle Three – Creative Intent

The creative intent of an attraction is nearly always related to the story or theme.

Here are a few examples of the creative intent of the some of the attractions in the park at Walt Disney World. These short descriptions appear in the park guide maps, and websites often convey (or at the very least hint at) the attractions' creative intent.

Big Thunder Mountain Railroad – Streak through a haunted gold-mining town aboard a rollicking runaway mine train.

Haunted Mansion – A spine-tingling tour through an eerie haunted house, home to ghosts, ghouls, and supernatural surprises.

Pirates of the Caribbean – Set sail on a swashbuckling voyage to a long-forgotten time and place when pirates and privateers ruled the seas.

Notice how most of these start with a verb, helping to set the stage for the experience (there's that word again!) the park guests will enjoy.

So, my little Bambi, how can you use this process to make your pet services appear more exciting, real and vitally important so your customers want to buy them now?

Here are a few examples:

Pack Leader Dog Adventure – A fun-filled canine expedition through the wilds of Sunderland, with beach swimming and wild agility sessions that leave your dog happy, satisfied and shattered!

24 Karat K9 Styling Session – A relaxing and re-invigorating gold standard groom that transforms your scruffy mutt into a pristine pooch.

Dazzling Doggy Day Care – A high-speed, exercise-filled, enriching and canine experience in our 100% safe hound haven. This will transform your bored stuck-at-home pooch into the happiest dog in town.

Creative Intent exercise – Now it's your turn!

What would be the creative intention for your main service? Fill in the blanks in this simple exercise below.

Describe ride/service ________________

Describe experience __________________

Filled with *what*? ____________________

Will leave the dog/client feeling *what*?

____

OK, now you're at the races. However, the creative intent doesn't just end with the name of the service.

Everything you do from that point on needs to be geared towards creating that experience for the clients.

Disney do this brilliantly at the Bibbidi Bobbidi Boutique.

This is where Fairy Godmothers Apprentices will pamper and primp your child until they look storybook stunning. Children can choose a hairstyle then add makeup, nail color and accessories—even a Disney Princess costume. (And little Princes have a 'Knight Package' option).

If you were taking notes during the pricing chapter, then it won't surprise you to learn they offer packages that range from $79 (a basic crown package) to $450 plus tax (the Princess Signature Dress Collection).

So, how do they get people queuing up to hand over money for what is essentially a kiddies' hair-style and a souvenir dress?

They do it by channelling their ***creative intent*** throughout the whole experience.

This begins with the sign at the entrance to the venue, where the wee kiddies awaiting their makeover believe that they are actually getting ready for Prince Charming's ball and Cinderella could show up any minute!

Many pet business owners make the mistake of not focusing all their efforts on the one thing they need to do to sell more services.

Steven Covey, author of *Seven Habits of Highly Effective People*, said, *'The main thing is to keep the main thing the main thing.'*

If your big hairy goal over the next quarter is to push a brand-new pet service, then EVERYTHING should be geared towards that one activity.

That means EVERYTHING.

All your videos.

All of your emails.

All your direct mail.

All your social media stuff.

Everyone in your 'feeder network' should know about it.

You should be gathering testimonials and repurposing them everywhere.

There should be an exciting 'pain point' filled page on your website devoted to it.

You should be texting clients to tell them about it, and asking them to refer dog-owning friends.

You can't say you are going to do something and then take part in activities that aren't going to contribute to the success of the project.

That is NOT behaviour congruent with achieving success.

Imagine what Seven Dwarfs Mine Train would look like if every five minutes the Imagineers working on the project were getting distracted by something they were seeing on Universal's social media page, or what the other Imagineers working in Animal Kingdom were doing.

It would be a total shitshow.

And if you are reading this thinking, *'But that's Disney. I don't have Cinderella's castle, I'm just a dog walker/groomer/trainer *insert pet profession*,'* then you, my friend, are completely missing the point.

Your number one priority…

Your most exciting project…

Your most important thing…

The best opportunity for success **is the thing you are working on right now.**

You need to channel your creative intent into the naming, designing, promoting and delivery of your pet business services.

In David Swartz's *The Magic of Thinking Big* he tells a story about three bricklayers.

A man walks past three men working on a building site.

He asks the first, '*What are you doing?*'

The first bricklayer replies, '*I'm laying bricks.*'

The second replies, '*I'm earning £9.50 an hour.*'

The third brick layer replies, '*I'm building a cathedral.*'

Are you building cathedrals or laying bricks in your pet business?

I've seen many pet business owners fail to make progress because they haven't been consistent when promoting their main service offering.

They are easily distracted by what their colleagues and competition are doing, which means they end up flitting between different projects and promotions, which makes it almost impossible to gain momentum and build a reputation around a particular specialisation.

Your head is probably buzzing with ideas for all the different services and experiences you can offer your clients, and that's a good thing, but I would urge you to pour all your energy and creative intent into the service offering that you can most easily promote to help you make the most money as quickly as you can.

Chapter Summary

Think creatively – When naming your pet business and your services, you should ignore what the majority of your competition are doing. If your aim is to have a standout pet business that towers above the competition then you need attention-grabbing service names that stand out like a Dalmatian at a pug party.

Think experience – Channel your creative intent into designing a whole experience that ties in with your service name. Don't be half-hearted with this. In 2011, I pioneered the industry with the invention of 'dog adventures'. It wasn't just a name though. The dog adventure experience shone through in the service offerings: we did hikes where the dogs wore back packs, as well as wild agility sessions and swimming lessons.

Think big and be bold – You'll benefit from doing a brainstorming session where you gather as many ideas as possible. Not all of these ideas will be immediately actionable, but because you are starting from a 'blue sky' position, you'll end up with a huge melting pot of ideas that will excite and inspire you to be bold with your marketing.

BONUS TRAINING – To watch a LIVE brainstorming session from one of my *Pet Business Bootcamps* where I show the attendees how to quickly come up with standout service names, AND get a FREE ***Storyselling Secrets Webinar*** from my Pet Business Profit Kickstarter programme, which will help you better connect with your ideal client and convert them into a customer, go to www.petbusinessmarketing.com/magicgift

Chapter Five

Peter Pan Promotions to Make Your Profits Fly

'Life's too short to always be serious.'

Goofy

As you reach the entrance to Disney's Magic Kingdom, you're so excited to arrive that you don't realise you've been walking up a slight incline ever since you got off the monorail or ferry (weirdly, I prefer the monorail).

And by the time you reach the iconic Cinderella's castle, you haven't noticed you are already at third-floor level, and you have no clue at all that you're standing on a hive of activity where there's a whole system of Disney tunnels underfoot.

I'm not just talking about a small cellar area where Captain Hook keeps his rum…this subterranean world occupies over 390,000 square feet of space underground.

There's a Cast Member (Disney-speak for staff) cafeteria called The Mouseketeria, a Cast Member hairdressing service called Kingdom Kutters, and The Glow Room where all the neon-lit Mickey ears, bracelets and swords sold in carts are stored.

In total there are nine acres of underworld tunnels in the form of a circle with spokes leading off in various directions.

The tunnel walls are colour coded to make it easier for Cast Members to navigate their way underneath the park to their desired location.

Why was this created?

Well, rumour has it that Walt Disney was wandering through Tomorrowland in Disneyland California when a Cast Member dressed as a cowboy walked by him on his way to his position at Frontierland.

One glance told Walt that a cowboy dressed in a checked shirt, bandana and cowboy boots twirling a six-shooter looked totally out of place in Tomorrowland.

This was supposed to be the future world and not the middle 1800s.

Walt racked his brain for a solution.

He didn't want anything distracting visitors from their magical experience.

How could his Cast Members be transported to their designated work stations *without* being seen by the general public?

An underground Disney was the solution.

This was an impossibility in Disneyland California which was too small. But the much larger Walt Disney World planned for Florida was a different story.

So, plans were hatched to build these Disney World tunnels (which would become known as Utilidors) under the new Magic Kingdom.

The projected cost of creating the Magic Kingdom was rumoured to be $4 million. The addition of the underworld tunnels raised that to $9 million.

And whilst the secret network is technically under the Magic Kingdom, it isn't actually underground. Due to Florida's high-water table, digging out a basement would have been practically impossible. Disney improvised by building the tunnels at ground level and creating the public world right on top.

Cool, eh?

What I really like about this story is Walt didn't get to implement this idea until the second Walt Disney World was built in Florida.

We've talked about how Walt used the term 'plussing' all the time. He was always looking for ways to 'plus' every experience to make it better and more memorable. Well, in this instance he plussed the whole park!

You've probably heard the phrase 'If it ain't broke, don't fix it,' but sometimes it's better to say, 'If it ain't broke, break it!'

See, it takes a lot of guts to change a business that is already successful. However, thinking of change as 'plussing' will help you remember that change means improvement.

Walt changed and improved the Californian Disney experience by 'plussing' it at the Florida Disney World.

However, you don't need to open a theme park or even start a new pet business to begin the process of changing (or plussing) the experience for your clients.

In fact, as we discussed in the last chapter, the best opportunity you have right now to improve your business's fortunes is the opportunity to change (and improve) your ***existing business and services***.

You have a unique opportunity right now to redesign your pet business processes, your promotions and your client experience, so you elevate it above the offerings of your crappy competition.

So, let's take an imaginary walk through a day at Disney, to see what lessons you can take from the experience and plug into your own business.

Usually, when you arrive at Disney you've endured a lot of hardship to get there.

You've scrimped and saved for a long time, months, maybe years, or even decades.

You've probably spent many long hours travelling hundreds or thousands of miles before you arrive at the park gates. Yet, despite all that you are delighted, if not ecstatic, to be there.

And though you've already invested thousands of pounds to get to the door of Disney you are more than happy, and are well prepared, to spend a lot of money while you are there.

All four times we visited Disneyland as a family, we had a budget we were intent on sticking to…but we ended up spending way more than planned, and we were more than happy to do so.

That's because Disney know what makes their clients happy, and what makes them buy stuff again and again and again.

They know it's not about the *transaction*, it's about the *experience*.

Most pet business owners think about their business in terms of individual sales.

How many walks, grooms, consultations, training sessions did we do today?

Very little effort goes into planning a series of amazing experiences that keep clients coming back, and buying more!

Creating an experience *matters*.

When you design your services to be a series of experiences that seamlessly flow from one to the other, then you'll keep your clients coming back time and time again. When you do this, you'll increase your lifetime customer value which means you need to spend less time and energy finding new clients.

Repeat business is a HUGE part of the Disney's success.

In fact, all successful businesses that have been around for a long time understand this, and they put a lot of effort and energy into building and maintaining fantastic relationships with their clients.

I once watched a documentary about The Savoy Hotel, London, and it said 50% of their business comes from repeat business and returning customers.

50%!

Imagine if every time you took on two new customers you knew one of them was going to stay with you for a very long time, maybe forever?

How predictable (and profitable) would your business be with that kind of guaranteed income?

So, the first takeaway from this chapter is to make sure your pet business is set up to facilitate repeat business.

Are you set up for repeat business?

Do you have services that clients can keep buying again and again and again?

If not, you need to change what you offer so can you add repeat sales, or even continuity, to your service offering.

Some pet services naturally lend themselves to repeat sales. I often joke that the only reason a dog walker or dog groomer should lose a client is if they lose or set fire to the dog.

Doggy day cares have a similar business model. Once you have a client then they should technically stay with you for years.

You can argue that the business model of dog trainers, animal therapists and pet photographers is more problematic because their business is set up to acquire a client, deliver the service and then the customer usually leaves, which means you have to find another customer to take their place.

However, there is a lot of competition for walkers, groomers and day cares also, so in reality there's a need for everyone to 'plus' the experience so you continually stand out from the crowd.

Here are two simple steps to increase the lifetime value of your repeat customers:

1. Make sure you have a service pyramid where clients are encouraged to buy packages instead of one-time sales, and where you have multiple services that ascend in price. That way you can move clients from one service to the next, or from one service to a more expensive service.
2. Create a client customer journey map that actually plans out (and shows the client) the pathway of services that they can (and should) use. Make sure you communicate this often using all types of media.

It's easy to get in your own way when it comes to selling, and the simple act of introducing a new service, and then communicating that to your customers, can have a HUGE impact on your pet business profits.

This is very simple to do.

You'll see on the next page the Pet Business Ladder of Success.

PBIC LADDER OF SUCCESS
ELITE MASTERMIND
PLATINUM SIX FIGURE PRIVATE COACHING
DIAMOND PRIVATE COACHING
PBIC GOLD MEMBERSHIP
THE ULTIMATE PET BUSINESS PLAN
Dominic Hodgson

This clearly lays out for my coaching clients what services are available and what order they should be consumed in.

These levels of service (in my case coaching programmes) have been designed to give the right amount of help and support to the client, based on their business/personal needs.

I also have other programmes/products that people can buy at any one time.

So, people can buy low-priced books and self-study courses, or they can invest a higher figure for intensive coaching programs like my *Walk Yourself Wealthy Business in a Box*, or they can join my *Elite Mastermind* or come to a Pet Business Bootcamp.

A business like mine NEEDS these different-priced offerings.

Why?

Well, because not everyone wants to buy all of the things I offer, all of the time.

Some people will buy everything, but most won't.

People have varying appetites for hard work, and some people have other things going on in their life that mean there are certain times when they can't, or don't want to, focus as much on the growth of their business.

However, this **doesn't** mean they don't need any help from me, so it benefits me and my clients to have different-priced service offerings that they can invest in on the way 'up' and on the way 'down' the service ladder.

Disney works a similar way.

The most profitable and desirable 'sale' for Disney would probably be when someone visits the parks. Disney's retention rate for first-time visitors is around 70% (GULP!), so for Disney, getting someone to a park has to be the ultimate sale, as it virtually guarantees that 7 in 10 visitors will come again, which equals locked-in repeat business.

And when visiting the parks, customers have an ascending scale of options to choose from that increase in price. This is like my service pyramid I talked about earlier.

So, you can stay in a low-priced hotel on site, a mid-priced option that gets you early access to the parks, or you can spend several thousand dollars on a two-night stay aboard the Star Wars Galactic Starcruiser Immersive Experience, and there are many other options in between.

Just like my coaching business, Disney offers different options for customers depending on how much they want to spend.

However, not everyone can afford to visit the parks every year (and some may never be able to afford it), but they can buy other things from Disney.

They can go to the cinema to watch Disney movies. They can visit the Disney store. They can buy Disney merchandise, subscribe to Disney+ or join the D23 club where they can keep up to date on what is going on inside the world of Disney, without actually visiting the parks.

All this enables the customer to experience that Disney magic and makes them feel like they are a part of the Disney tribe all year round. For Disney, it massively increases the lifetime value of each customer.

Now, you might be reading this thinking, *'Well, I'm not Disney, and I'm not Dom either. I don't have all these different things I can offer my clients!'*

That might well be true, but there's no reason why you can't start adding more options to your service menu *right now*.

Most pet businesses don't do this.

Most pet businesses don't have different levels of service. They don't have special seasonal services or specific offers, for specialised walks, grooms, training sessions or time-limited offerings that they only sell at certain times throughout the year.

They simply offer the same services at the same price right throughout the year.

Which I shouldn't need to tell you is…

B

O

R

I

N

G

As well as adding new rides and attractions, Disney have special themes they run throughout the year, every year.

So, in spring they run Easter celebrations featuring fun activities like Candy Scrambles, character meet-and-greets with an Easter twist, and, of course, everyone's favourite Egg Hunt.

Many gift shops in Disney resorts have even offered pre-made Easter baskets for purchase. Usually, there is also a Cast Member on hand so you can build your own if you're looking for specific goodies for someone in particular.

Halloween is a three-month celebration of all things spooky. There's the Boo-to-you Halloween-themed Parade, Trick or Treating throughout the park, and Disney's Not-So-Spooky Spectacular fireworks display.

Every aspect of the park gets a Halloween twist, from the Halloween décor adorning the lampposts, to the iconic giant pumpkins outside Main Street Station. Even the famous Dapper Dans at Magic Kingdom get in on the act as they are taken over by their undead alter egos The Cadaver Dans — these spooky incarnations of the popular Main Street U.S.A. performers are dressed in ghoulish costumes and put on a spooktacular performance for guests.

And of course, there's Christmas. Most people go crazy at Christmastime anyway (me included – I LOVE Christmas), but Disney visitors in particular have a lot to get excited about. Each park has its own iconic Christmas tree, the Jungle Cruise becomes the Jingle Cruise, there's Mickey's Once Upon a Christmastime Parade, as well as LOTS of Christmas merchandise and goodies to consume, including Christmas Cookie Sundaes, Mickey Cinnamon Rolls and of course a Holiday Sandwich (oven-roasted turkey, stuffing, gravy and cranberry sauce on rustic bread).

We've had hundreds of great examples of PBIC members who have thrown themselves into the holiday spirit and put on a seasonal promotion that has wowed their long-term clients, caused money to pour into their bank accounts and brought new curious customers through the door.

Phil Houston who runs Tails of the Lake ran a Valentine's doggy date night.

Katie Guastapaglia got into the Easter spirit and dressed as the Easter bunny when she ran a hugely successful Easter promotion for her Scentventure membership.

Becky Oldfield of Contented Gundogs did an amazing Halloween promotion that included doggy 'grave digging' activities.

And Tim Jackson, who runs Pet2Impress, the UK's greatest day care, created his own nativity film, starring his staff and day care dogs!

Here are a final few takeaways about running these types of promotions.

- They are very easy to do. SO EASY! You just take any existing human activity/promotion and put a canine twist on it, and you're ready!

- Customers expect this kind of thing. They've been conditioned to look for them and invest in a seasonal promotion. Most of them buy Easter eggs, Halloween-themed washing powder and Christmas-themed kitchen roll, so trust me, they'll invest in a fun seasonal promotion for their dog!

- It's not cheesy, it's FUN! Don't think your customers are too sophisticated for this kind of silliness. They are NOT. And, if you market your promotion correctly, you'll find they are super profitable, and provide an easy and predictable income boost for your pet business, at regular intervals throughout the year.

A bit like building a warm email list will enable you to get new clients whenever you want, by simply sending an email. So, these promotions will enable you to make more money whenever you want, by simply sending out the promotion to your clients.

You'll send out the promotion and back comes more money, as reliable as a homing pigeon returning to his coop.

Finally, whilst these promotions aren't quite evergreen, they can be used year after year, again and again, with little change in the actual promotion.

These types of seasonal promotions are a great way to test what your clients want and are willing to spend more money on. Then you can use the results to help you design higher-priced levels of service.

So, what are you waiting for?

Go forth and design your Disney-style promotional calendar and sell more services!

Chapter Summary

Repeat Business Rocks – Finding and acquiring new clients is the most time-consuming, energy-sapping and expensive part of promoting your pet business, so you need to set up your business so you keep as many of them as you can. One way to ensure people stay clients longer – and keep buying from you – is to offer higher-priced services they can invest in.

Your Customer Map – When you arrive at Disney there are maps everywhere that tell you where you are now, and they direct you to the next exciting experience. You can increase lifetime customer value by creating a service map that shows your clients what they should buy from you next. Use online and offline media to communicate your customer map.

Create Exciting Experiences – All successful businesses understand that clients need to be excited and engaged or they'll be tempted to sample what the competition are offering. You can ensure your customers are never temped to check out your competitors by doing seasonal promotions that are fun and profitable.

BONUS TRAINING: Pet Business Paper and Ink Swipe File . To help inspire you to create some standout, memorable offline marketing materials, I've put together a swipe file of some amazing paper and ink marketing promotions I've collected over the years. These are real-life examples of how companies in different industries, and me and my private clients, have used paper and ink to improve and enhance the customer experience. There are 10 short videos in total, and you can see all of them by going to www.petbusinessmarketing.com/magicgift

Conclusion

Time to Magic Feather Your Marketing

'Don't just fly, soar.'

Dumbo

Two days before Christmas in 1986, Jeannie Yeager and Burt Rutan completed a 26,000-mile flight around the world without stopping or refuelling.

They returned to a hero's welcome and spent several weeks touring the USA to celebrate their achievement.

Around six months later, they were having dinner with friends Michael and Jane Eisner. Michael was the head honcho at Disney at the time.

Making small talk, Jane asked the obvious question after such an achievement:

'What are you doing next?'

Their reply was surprising:

'We're going to Disneyland.'

Jane turned to her husband and said, *'Michael, you've got to use that.'*

As a result, in 1987 Disney began featuring adverts after great sports events like the Super Bowl and the World Series.

The hero of the hour would be caught walking off the field. An off-screen narrator would pop the question:

'Now that you've won, what are you going to do next?' The hero would reply, *'I'm going to Disneyland!'*

This campaign has run for the last 30 years and is arguably one of Disney's greatest and most memorable advertising campaigns.

Disney harnessed the power of celebrities like Tom Brady, Michael Jordan, Bruce Springsteen, and even Santa Claus, and by using winners from baseball, NASCAR, the Olympics, Miss America and *American Idol*, they managed to establish Disneyland as 'THE' destination of choice across diverse and niche areas of American culture.

Over time they've also created an association that going to Disney is something 'winners' do.

That's a very powerful idea, and I can testify that, rightly or wrongly, when Beth and I took the boys to Orlando, we both felt like winners, and that was without us even seeing the advertising campaign!

'We did it honey, we got the bairns to Disney!'

This idea of 'place' is important in marketing.

When you build a business, you aren't just creating products and services; you're actually creating a place in people's minds.

The stories you tell in your marketing massively influence how dog owners in your town 'think' about your business.

You want them saying stuff like:

'You need a dog groomer? Then you must get in touch with Kirsty Jackson, she's the best in the North West...'

Or:

'You need a puppy trainer? Then you must contact Karen Boyce, she's the best puppy trainer in Wales…'

By implementing the five magic marketing spells in this book you'll start transforming your pet business from being seen as average and ordinary, to being known as exceptional and extraordinary.

I can't guarantee it will happen overnight, but it will happen if you stick to the plan.

How can you move forward faster and virtually guarantee success?

For that you need a magic feather…

The Magic Feather

The summer of 2013 was a good one. Business was good, and the sun was out almost every day. This was especially enjoyable for us dog walkers, as it meant shorts, T-shirts, sunglasses and sunblock instead of wellies, Barbours and woolly hats, but it presented some challenges with the dogs.

The main one was how to keep them cool. It probably won't surprise you to know that most of our clients like their dogs to be walked around at lunchtime as this is slap bang in the middle of the time they are out of the house at work. This is also the warmest part of the day. Now being in the Northeast of England, this isn't usually a problem, but this was the warmest, driest summer for several years, so it was not the ideal time of the day to be exercising any dog.

Fortunately, in Sunderland we are blessed with many beautiful beaches, and we generally spend a lot of time playing with and training the dogs there. We also have a lot of dogs who love the water, and that year I had set myself a challenge to teach all the dogs to swim that couldn't already. I'm a firm believer in getting hands-on with all my dog training, and so I knew the best way for me to help the dogs to swim was to get in the water with them. However, even in a hot summer, the sea is pretty cold here, so we found a nice quiet man-made lake that I could easily spend a bit of time in without my lily-white legs turning blue.

We had a lot of fun that summer and successfully managed to get almost all of the dogs to enjoy swimming, or at least to feel more comfortable in the water. I say almost, because there were a few that either weren't very keen or were just not really suited to swimming, like Nell the Samoyed, who has a very thick and heavy coat.

One summer's day, we arrived at our usual spot at the lake and started to play with the dogs, and this is the day when the penny dropped for me about how powerful it can be to find a dog's kryptonite.

The area near to where we were playing in the water had evidently been privy to some kind of fox attack on a swan the previous day, and one of our party, little Stuey the Pug, was taking a very keen interest in the scene of the swan massacre, which was now strewn with swan feathers. Now Stuey the Pug is a lovely little guy that is always a pleasure to walk. He isn't much into playing with toys, but he always stays close by us unless we go in the water. He isn't very keen on swimming, despite our previous efforts.

Today he was Chief Inspector Stu, and try as I might, I couldn't get him to come away from the crime scene. I tried treats and toys but to no avail. Even when we moved further round the lake, he kept trying to head back to the same spot. So just when I thought, *'That's it; he's going to have to go on lead today,'* I remembered the words of my good friend and dog training mentor, David Davies: *'To get a dog's attention you need to be able to reward him with something that he is interested in at the time.'*

OK then, I thought; if Stuey wants a feather, then Stuey can have a feather. But he will have to follow me to get it.

Would this work?

I wasn't really sure to be honest, and my assistant looked at me like I was a little mad. I went and found the biggest (and cleanest) swan feather I could and got

Stuey's attention with it. This wasn't too difficult. Then I played with him with the feather, and I teased him a little just the same way I would with a normal dog toy. By now Stuey was very interested in the feather, so much so I was able to back away from him, and he followed me.

Using the feather, I managed to lure him back to where the others were, and I have to admit I was feeling rather pleased. I then began to wonder what I could get Stuey to do for this feather. Well, I was already wet, so I began to edge my way into the lake slowly. And Stuey followed. He was a bit tentative at first, but he took a step or two into the water. I continued to go deeper, and whenever Stuey looked like he was losing interest, I would wave the feather around and let him have a sniff or a little bite of the feather. I went deeper until the water was now up above my knees, and Stuey was almost fully submerged. This was it. I moved back further still so the water rose up to my waist, and lo and behold, that little pug pushed off and started swimming towards me, freestyle.

Well, needless to say, I couldn't believe it, and I'm not sure Stuey could either. He swam for a few minutes, and we repeated this exercise a few more times using the feather as the temporary kryptonite at the time.

That story really did happen, and it first appeared in my debut book *How to Be Your Dog's Superhero.*

But I obviously lifted 'the magic feather' idea from the Disney classic *Dumbo.*

You'll remember in the movie, after a night on the beer, Dumbo mysteriously awakens atop a tall tree. Let's be honest, we've all been there after a heavy night on the grog…

Dumbo's friend Timothy mouse gets the idea that he flew up the tree using his giant elephant ears to do so.

After much mocking, Jim Crow advises Timothy to manipulate Dumbo to try flying using a 'Magic Feather' as motivation.

After a successful test flight, Dumbo and Timothy plan on surprising the audience by flying in the middle of a fall, but as they plummet to earth, Dumbo loses the Magic Feather, temporarily losing his motivation. Timothy reveals to Dumbo that the feather was just a gag, and at the last minute, Dumbo manages to fly without it.

I see a lot of pet business owners fail to reach their potential because they are constantly searching for a Magic Feather they think is going to solve all of their pet business problems.

They chase validation and verification by constantly collecting 'badges' of merit from dog training associations and industry peer groups, or they plug into silly social-media-obsessed gooroos who wave alluring content calendars like the apple the wicked queen gives to Snow White (*temptingly tasty, but secretly deadly*).

If I just get one more accreditation, then I'll know enough to be able to increase my prices.

If I only get better at blogging, I'll be a success.

All of my friends are attending that 72-hour virtual dog conference, so I HAVE to go too.

I have a spare few hundred quid in my account, I better get a new logo/website/dog washer/van.

Those aren't Magic Feathers. They are *Fake Feather* activities that fool you into thinking you need them so you can make your pet business fly.

Over the last six years I've mentored hundreds of pet business owners, and I've found there are usually a small number (maybe even just one or two) of activities that you need to do right now to move your business forward.

How to turn your pet business around?

If you're starting out in your pet business then the key is to nail your niche and your message, and then get the word 'out there' that your pet business exists. You should use all the online and offline media that your ideal client will see/hear. This means that as well as building a website and using social media, you need to get off your ass and put leaflets/postcards/newsletters in dog owners' hands in your town.

If you are an established pet business who is growing with momentum, then it's about maximising profit and creating systems to sustain that growth. When your business improves and your diary starts to fill up, you tend to forget about the basics like increasing prices, introducing upsells, encouraging referrals, etc. You need systems and procedures that enable you to grow as big as your ambition allows. Don't get so busy working 'in' your pet business that you forget to work 'on' it.

If your business is full to bursting and you're fully systemised then you probably feel like it's time to explore new opportunities in – or even outside of – the pet industry. Finding the 'business within the business' is the most exciting thing for an entrepreneur because you get to put all the lessons you've learned into a new venture. You usually grow your second business much faster than you did the first, and often the second (or third, or fourth) business ends up being way more profitable and enjoyable than your first business. That is certainly what happened with me.

I started out in 2011 with the launch of Pack Leader Dog Adventures, the UK's first dog adventure company. I quickly added luxury home boarding, then dog training to my service menu. I hosted events and then became a published author. I've been a podcaster, a speaker, I've written more books, created online dog training programmes and memberships, and now I primarily help coach other pet business owners through my Pet Business Inner Circle membership, business development programmes and high-level Masterminds.

My wife Beth supported me when I first started my business, and in 2020 after 20 years as a teacher she was able to leave that profession and join the business full-time as my Operations Manager. Since 2015 my eldest son Alex has been Adventure Manager, and he now runs Pack Leader Dog Adventures.

There have been a few bumps along the road, but I have built my dream pet business, and I've been able to fund that growth by implementing the marketing advice I've shared in this book.

Now it's time for you to take your pet business in a new and exciting direction.

First you fix your existing business, and you can use any of the five marketing spells in this book to prime the promotional pump, so you can drive up demand, sell more services and make more money from your amazing service.

1. Add 'WOW' Factor to Your Service
2. Give Your Hero Pet Business a Vicious Villain
3. Add the Prince Charming Factor to Your Premium Prices
4. Storysell Your 5-Star Service
5. Peter Pan Your Promotions

Then, once you've fixed what you've got, you can start planning the next phase of your business success.

The pet industry is unlike any other profession, and you have a unique opportunity to build a profitable business that is a vehicle for all the amazing experiences you want in life.

If you want this to happen in your pet business then you need to stop flitting from one bright shiny object to another like a stoned Tinkerbell, stick to the fundamentals and **TAKE ACTION**.

To help you take that next step, and more easily implement the strategies I've laid out in this book, I have a FREE Magic Gift which will enable you to quickly move forward and get results FAST!

Turn the page to claim your FREE Magic Gift.

MY FREE GIFT TO YOU

Claim five powerful, profit-boosting free gifts now.

I want this book to represent a fresh and exciting start for your pet business.

Like you, I've read loads of books, but most of them get shelved as soon as I've finished.

In my life there have only been a dozen or so books that I've enjoyed enough for me to want to read them again.

More importantly, I've only read a handful of books that have inspired me to take action on the content once I'd finished.

I want this to be one of those books for you, and my mission now is to get you to take action on what you have learned in *Pet Business Marketing Magic.*

Your pet business should be too important to you not to take action and start implementing the marketing secrets I have shared with you. I know for a fact (because I have done it myself) that you will be making more money a lot faster once you actually *do* take action.

So, to help you get started, I have five FREE special gifts for you.

1. **Magic Gift number 1** – FREE ***How to Disnify Your Pet Business*** audiobook! This is the full unedited audio version of this book, but you get more than me

just reading *How to Disnify Your Pet Business.* In this exclusive audio I also go off topic and add in even more secrets and examples that show you how you can master the magic marketing spells. You can get immediate access to this amazing bonus by going to: www.petbusinessmarketing.com/magicgift

2. **Magic Gift number 2** – To help you better tap into your ideal client's fears, frustrations and failures, I am giving you FREE access to a special 60-minute audio training that I've only previously shared with my *Diamond* private coaching clients – In ***Seven Psychological Sales Triggers*** you'll discover how to easily connect with more dog owners about their pooch problems. This will transform the effectiveness of your website copy, social media posts and any other articles and sales pieces you produce. To claim this FREE resource now, go to:
www.petbusinessmarketing.com/magicgift

3. **Magic Gift number 3 – *Pet Business Paper and Ink Swipe File*.** To help inspire you to create some standout, memorable offline marketing materials, I've put together a swipe file of some amazing paper and ink marketing promotions I've collected over the years. These are real-life examples of how companies in different industries, and me and my private clients, have used paper and ink to improve and enhance the customer experience. There are 10 short videos in total, and you can see all of them by going to www.petbusinessmarketing.com/magicgift

4. **Magic Gift number 4** – To watch a LIVE brainstorming session from one of my *Pet Business Bootcamps* where I show the attendees how to quickly

come up with standout service names, AND get a FREE ***Storyselling Secrets Webinar*** from my Pet Business Profit Kickstarter programme, which will help you better connect with your ideal client and convert them into a customer, go to www.petbusinessmarketing.com/magicgift

5. **Magic Gift number 5** – To help you effortlessly add more value to your pet business without even taking on a single new client, I'm giving you FREE access to my ***Unbelievable Pet Business Upsells Masterclass***. In this exclusive training I'll show you how to effortlessly add higher-priced services to your existing service menu. You'll be able to plug these upsell ideas straight into your service offering so you can make more money from your existing clients. To claim this FREE resource now, go to www.petbusinessmarketing.com/magicgift

You have in your hands a blueprint for success. There really is no excuse for you not to take one (or all) of these free resources to further build on what you have learned so far.

The information in each one of these free gifts has the power to transform your pet business, but if you implement all of them, you have the potential to put your business growth on steroids.

How far you take your pet business is up to you.

Is this going to be a hobby business that just pays the bills, or will it be the premium, profitable and fun pet business empire you want it to be?

To answer that question and get more help from me, go to www.petbusinessmarketing.com/magicgift

If you have trouble accessing any of these resources, then email Beth at hello@packleaderdogadventures.co.uk and she will be happy to sort it out.

Thanks for reading.

Keep it unreal.

Dom Hodgson

ACKNOWLEDGEMENTS

Pet Business Marketing Magic is my ninth book overall, and I hope you have as much fun reading it as I did writing it.

You'll know all about my business story by now, and you'll know it's been full of ups and downs, but overall, I've had way more successes than failures, and I've certainly had a LOT of fun!

That is partly down to my 'get shit done' attitude, but it's also due to the company I keep, and the people I surround myself with. That leads me to the next bit of advice I have for you.

Don't let anyone tell you that you can't do anything in your business. If you've surrounded yourself with negative Nellies who drag you down like crabs in a bucket, then it's time to get some new friends.

The great Jim Rohn said, *'You are the average of the six people you hang around with'*, and I truly believe the quickest way for you to 'level up' your thinking, and your attitude to success, is to start hanging around with people who have achieved, or who are achieving, the kind of things you want to experience with your business.

I have an awesome team around me, and I wouldn't be here with them, so here's my acknowledgments to the people who help me keep moving forward.

First and always first comes my family.

Beth, my beautiful wife and Operations Manager, is by my side in everything I do, and I wouldn't get half (or even a quarter) of it done without her constant support. Toby and Alex are the best boys a dad could ask for and always make me proud (we have a great laugh too).

Alex also does an amazing job as the Adventure Operations Manager running Pack Leader Dog Adventures, which is the adventure and boarding side of our business.

My Mam and Dad are always there to help me and Beth with the kids, dogs and the business, so thanks again to you two. X

Thanks to Mr Disney Customer Service himself, Vance Morris, for his guidance and support since I started this book.

Thanks to real-life Imagineer Jim Sarno, for his wisdom and insights into the Imagineering process.

Thanks also to my good friend and resident expert for all things video, Alex 'the video guy' Wardle. Alex takes care of all my podcasts, events and online training videos.

Thanks to Nick Jones from Full Media Ltd for proofreading this and my other books.

Huge thanks to my tribe of loyal, kick-ass pet business owners and private coaching clients inside the Pet Business Inner Circle, especially my *Elite* members. You guys all rock!

And finally, thanks to you, my friend, for buying, reading and hopefully actioning this book!

OK, you are done. This is the end.

Well not quite, because now you need to claim your free Magic Gifts, which will help you plug all this powerful, proven marketing advice straight into your pet business.

Remember, you can get access to the five FREE Marketing Magic Gifts by going
to www.petbusinessmarketing.com/magicgift

ABOUT THE AUTHOR

Dom Hodgson is a pet business pioneer, expert dog trainer and bestselling author. He's also widely recognised as the world's leading pet business coach and marketing strategist.

With his eldest son, Alex, he runs the UK's number-one dog adventure company, Pack Leader Dog Adventures. Since 2011, PLDA has been helping dog owners in Sunderland have more fun and less stress with their dogs. Dom innovated the dog adventure concept that for the first time provided a safe, stimulating, five-star experience for dog owners who wanted more than just a walk around the block.

In 2016, Dom wrote the bestselling book, *How To Be Your Dog's Superhero,* which is available to buy on Amazon Kindle, as an audiobook on Audible or you can get a signed copy (and a special free gift) by going to www.petbusinessmarketing.com/books. This was followed by *Walk Yourself Wealthy*,*Worry Free Walks*, *The Perfect Puppy Project*, and *Rescue Dog Rehoming Remedies.*

Pet Business Marketing Magic is the third pet business book in the 'Grow Your Pet Business FAST!' series. To find out more about Dom's other books, courses and pet business coaching you should go to www.petbusinessmarketing.com

Dom is an international speaker and teaches pet dog owners how to have more fun with, and get more control of, their dogs, and he teaches pet business owners how to have more fun, and make more money, in their business.

To enquire about booking Dom to speak at an event, you should email Beth on hello@packleaderdogadventures.co.uk

Dom lives in Town Farm with his wife Beth, youngest son Toby, their two dogs Sid the Cocker and Derek the Dogue de Bordeaux, and eight chickens.

Other Books by the Author

Pet Business Books

Walk Yourself Wealthy: The quick, easy and no-BS guide to transform your passion for pooches into an insanely profitable and fun dog-walking empire

The Ultimate Pet Business Plan: How to launch, grow, staff, scale and dominate your local town with an outrageously profitable, impactful and fun pet business

Pet Business Marketing Magic: The secrets to transform your boring, bashful, broke business into a bold, brilliant, booming beast of an operation

Dog Training Books

How to Be Your Dog's Superhero: Transform your dastardly dog using the power of play

Worry Free Walks: How to transform your difficult, dangerous and devilish dog into a problem-free pooch you are proud to take to the park

The Perfect Puppy Recipe: The ultimate no-mess, zero-stress, step-by-step guide to raising the perfect puppy

The Dog Owner's Self-Isolation Survival Guide: Discover how to quickly and easily exercise, entertain and emotionally connect with your dog from the seclusion of your sitting room

The Lazy Dog Owners' Ten Minute Training Plan: The quick, easy and no-BS guide to turn your dastardly dog into a perfect pooch

Rescue Dog Rehoming Remedies Volume One: Eleven dog training secrets and stories from the world's leading rescue dog trainers

All books can be purchased from all major online retailers in eBook, print and audio format.

To purchase direct from the author please go to www.petbusinessmarketing.com

Disney PBICasaurus

Some more mouse-inspired marketing magic…

Leave it outside the berm – The 'berm' is a dirt wall that surrounds many Disney parks (particularly castle parks such as the Magic Kingdom at Walt Disney World) with the goal of visually separating the outside world from the fantasy and adventure within. This visual barrier also has an emotional impact. Entering one of the Disney parks can fill you with excitement, anticipation, joy and wonder…but it also gives you the ability to leave behind things that are hindering you and dragging you down. For a period of time, you are able to leave those things 'outside the berm'.

If your pet business service is experiential, then the dogs will be excited to work with you, and your clients will crave the 'feel good' factor you give them. Your service will not only impact their dog's life, it will actually make the client feel deeply connected to you and your business.

Magic band – This is the electronic wristband that contains your park ticket, room key, FastPass reservations, and more. You can even use it for purchases in the parks and hotels.

Could your clients receive a 'magic collar' as part of their 'onboarding' process, that gives their dog special privileges and perks?

Park hopper – A ticket that allows a guest admission to more than one park in the same day.

Could you employ a hopper-type system in your pet business that enables clients to mix and match services?

Yes, you could! Are you offering these kinds of services already, but maybe you don't advertise it or charge extra for the privilege? Maybe you should…

Pixie dust – As any Neverland fan knows, within Disney lore pixie dust is a magical glittery substance that gives fairies and people the ability to fly, and it creates other magical effects when applied. Pixie dust moments are arranged and happen to lucky guests each and every day. Being selected as Family of the Day at the Magic Kingdom, or getting selected to partake in a show or attraction, are some examples of these pre-arranged moments. Others are random acts like being given a dessert or being moved to front row seats in a show.

How can you sprinkle some pet business pixie dust on your client's experience?

Very Merry Unbirthday – An event celebrated on any or all days of the year which are not a person's birthday, made famous in Disney's *Alice in Wonderland* when the Mad Hatter and the March Hare celebrate a very merry unbirthday party.

You can create unlimited promotional 'unbirthdays' in your business. You don't need to wait for your business birthday, a special 'dog day' or Easter, Halloween or Christmas. You can sellabrate (see what I did there…celebrate/sell) whenever you like!

EMH – Extra Magic Hours – Extra Magic Hours are extended theme park hours available to Disney World Resort hotel guests. On certain days of the week, guests can enter a park one hour earlier or stay in a park up to two hours later than normal park operating hours. This is a 'perk' of staying in a Disney World Resort hotel.

What 'perks' can you come up with for your best clients that will make them feel special and appreciated?

FastPass – A Disney FastPass allows you to plan your visit to the parks in advance AND enables you to 'skip the line' on the three rides per day, potentially saving you hours of waiting time. Remember, people will pay more to get preferential treatment that saves time.

How can you implement a FastPass type system in your pet business?

Forced perspective – How does Disney make the centrepiece of the Magic Kingdom, Cinderella Castle, appear bigger than it is? Well, the first floor of Cinderella Castle is built to scale, while the second storey is built smaller! The second storey has windows and blocks that are five eighths the size of those on the first floor, while the castle's top spire is roughly half the size that it appears to be.

By using this forced perspective, Disney are tricking your eyes into perceiving the upper levels of their buildings to be much bigger than they really are.

You can employ similar marketing 'tricks' to make your business seem bigger, better and more desirable than it otherwise might appear, and certainly 'better' than your competition.

Having a monthly newsletter, putting on an event, or writing a book would be good examples of how you can make your pet business seem bigger, better and more impressive than your competition.

Plussing – This was a famous Walt Disney maxim, and how he inspired people to make ideas even better.

When working on Snow White, the first full-length animated movie, he asked his staff to keep thinking of ways they could make it even better. If someone brought him a drawing or design, he would ask them, 'How can we plus it?'

This became part of the ethos at the parks and hotels and has helped Disney build a reputation for world-class customer service and a once-in-a-lifetime experience.

Why not implement an ABP (Always Be Plussing) culture in your pet business, where all team members are encouraged to keep thinking of ways of plussing the customer experience?

Cast Member – Disney employees are called Cast Members. Visitors are called guests. When Cast Members are anywhere they can be seen by the public, they are 'onstage' and must remain in character.

At Pack Leader Dog Adventures, we don't have dog walkers, we have *Canine Fulfilment Officers.*

Walkers 'walk' a dog. We do much more than that with our adventures.

Changing a name is the easiest way to differentiate yourself from the competition. Make sure your pet business 'Cast Members' are appropriately named too.

Free Chapter of *The Ultimate Pet Business Plan*

Introduction

'A goal without a plan is just a wish.'

Antoine de Saint-Exupéry

Three fish lived in a pond. One was named 'Plan ahead', another was 'Think fast' and the third was called 'Wait and see'.

Weird names, I know, but work with me here…

One morning they heard a fisherman say he would be casting his net in their pond the next day.

'Plan ahead' said, 'I am swimming down the river and heading to the sea tonight.'

'Think fast' said, 'With my lightning-quick thinking, I'm sure to come up with a plan when I need to.'

'Wait and see' lazily said, 'I can't be bothered to think about it now.'

The next day came around and, sure enough, the fisherman cast his net in the pond.

By this time 'Plan ahead' had already made his way far away from danger, and was safe in the ocean.

But 'Think fast' and 'Wait and see' were caught by the fisherman.

True to his name, 'Think fast' quickly rolled onto his belly, went limp, closed his eyes and pretended to be dead. 'Bugger, this fish is no good!' said the fisherman and threw him safely back into the water.

However, 'Wait and see' was caught, killed and ended up on a plate with some chips and mushy peas.

That is why people say, 'In times of danger, when the net is cast, plan ahead or plan to think fast.'

A fishy story for sure, but there's a good reason I'm starting this book with a poisson-filled parable.

When starting a new business, or when you are expanding or going in a new direction with an established business, it always pays to plan ahead.

Why you need a business plan.

As a business owner, you'll find there's always a dangerous net ready to be cast over your operation.

This net takes many forms.

It could be your ever-growing competition who are always hungrily eyeing up your assets as they try to pilfer your customers.

It might be the ever-changing business environment. The pet services sector has undergone some huge changes in the last ten years, and the next ten are set to be just as unpredictable.

Or it could be your own indifference, laziness or lack of imagination which causes your pet business to falter.

Trust me, if you aren't constantly thinking of new ways to promote your services, that excite your prospects and thrill your clients, then their head will be turned by someone else.

How do you prevent this happening to your business?

By planning, of course – and, just as importantly, taking action…

The dictionary definition of plan is: a detailed proposal for doing or achieving something.

The Ultimate Pet Business Plan will, if you follow it closely, help you to achieve something special. It will enable you to build a pet business that attracts the best clients, earn a fantastic income, and allow you to make a tremendous impact in your canine community.

That last point is worth touching on:

I've had three different businesses within the pet industry, I've written four books on the subject, and I've met and mentored hundreds of passionate pet business owners over the last eight years.

I know you want your business to be the vehicle that brings you and your family everything you deserve.

I also know you aren't in this 'just for the money'. I know you are passionate about helping people, bringing dogs and their owners closer together, and generally improving the welfare of dogs in your community, with your amazing services.

The uncomfortable truth which most failing pet business owners ignore is that the best way to make a bigger impact with your services, so you can help more dogs and their owners, is to get better at marketing.

The business who delivers an amazing service and presents that service better than anyone else usually ends up on top.

Mastering how to effectively market your services will enable you to build a kick-ass profitable pet business, that attracts the best high-fee-paying clients, touches more people and has a bigger influence in your community.

My 'plan' is for this book to reach out and resonate with the small number of truly ambitious dog walkers, trainers, groomers, doggy day care owners, and those just about to start a business (or if you are just thinking about starting a pet business). And anyone else in this amazing industry who is already offering life-changing services but who lacks the marketing skills to successfully promote their services, and is sick of working long hours with little or no reward.

I'll be sharing my proven marketing methods that will help you claim your place at the top of the mountain, and be recognised as the premier pet professional in your town, country, or even the world…

However, as important as planning is, you shouldn't plan so much that you forget to take action.

As the great Napoleon Hill said, 'Plan your work, and work your plan!'

'I'm working on my business plan' should be something you say once, then action until it's done.

Actions speak louder than words.

Have you heard the following statement from a friend or relative:

'This year I'm going to…lose weight, run a marathon, write a book, take a once-in-a-lifetime holiday' or any other activity you can imagine.

Usually, their plans involve simply talking about an activity. Rarely if ever do they transfer to the action phase required to actually achieve anything.

There's knowing what you need to do to achieve success, and then there's actually getting off your ass and fucking doing something about it.

If you are a dreamer, a thinker, a procrastinator and an 'avoider' then please return this book and I'll happily send you a refund.

This book is for the 'doers' who aren't 100% sure how to do something but will have a go anyway.

Prepare to be astonished.

You'll find a lot of the ideas I'm going to share with you will be new, different, unorthodox and may even fill you with fear…

That's because they will force you to step outside of your comfort zone, and develop into a new kind of business owner.

Rest assured, though, that The Ultimate Pet Business Plan is a proven, practical plan of action that will hold your hand and walk you through the three phases of your pet business growth.

The phases are: launching and establishing your new business, systemising and scaling and expanding, and innovating, reinventing and dominating.

Who is this book is for?

This book is for any service-based sector in the pet industry.

I primarily coach dog walkers, trainers and groomers, but I've also given business-changing advice to doggy day care owners, pet photographers, field owners and even pet scanners. When you practise and understand, as I do, how proper marketing works, then you can apply effective marketing principles to any pet business.

If you've bought this book I assume you're thinking of starting a pet business, have just started one, or you have an established business you wish to expand and scale (but don't know how).

I'll be sharing with you how to best position and market your business so you can make the biggest impact possible. If you've already created a great pet business, and now you've hit a bit of a wall with your growth and are out of ideas, then I will give you some options in terms of how you can innovate and expand in a new direction and, if you wish, even re-invent your business entirely.

So, what makes me so qualified to teach you how to market your pet business? Well, I'm not some jumped up gooroo who has done an MBA in general marketing and then jumped into the pet business sector because its looks like a 'hot market'. Nor am I a dog walker who has built a business by charging low prices, who now has 3,000 Twitter followers, a Facebook group with 2,000 members, and now thinks that qualifies me to teach other pet business owners about business.

So, who the hell am I? Good question, let's get to know each other a bit.

I'm Dom Hodgson, father of two boys, Alex (26) and Toby (18), and husband of Beth (a schoolteacher who wouldn't let me share her age, and quite right too.) I own two dogs, a cocker spaniel called Sid and a Dogue de Bordeaux called Derek, and six chickens (my favourite chicken Sharon passed away while I was finishing this book; more on my chickens later…). Most importantly, I've run my own multi-faceted pet business since 2011.

My pet business journey.

I started out as a dog runner, then I pioneered the introduction of dog adventures. In 2012 I became a dog trainer, then I ran an online dog store, I've since written three dog training books, two pet business books and created dozens of online courses, and I've also hosted two dog podcasts.

I've built a reputation that has enabled me to speak in front of hundreds of pet business owners at seminars all over the UK. Since 2017 I've run intensive marketing bootcamps for pet business owners, and in 2019 I created the first pet business super-conference A.K.A. IMPACT. For the last three years I've primarily mentored other pet business owners, to help them grow their business faster than their competition.

I'm not telling you any of this to brag (honest!), but rather to show you that over the last eight years I've tried lots of different things in my business.

Not all of my ventures have been successful, and I'll be sharing my low points with you too.

But I've enjoyed every step along the way, my businesses have always been profitable, and over the last eight years I've gradually created my own dream business that enables me to write, teach, mentor and work with amazing business owners.

It's likely that your dream pet business will be a lot different to mine, and that's how it should be. You shouldn't want to copy me or anyone else.

You might not want to write a book or stand on a stage and speak to an audience, any more than I want to learn how to groom or massage a dog.

What you can and definitely should do, however, is 'model' your business on the success principles I lay out in this book.

See, much like the principles of dog training, the principles of successful marketing never change.

So, it doesn't matter whether you want to dominate your town with your dog walking business, have dreams to become the number one puppy trainer, own a string of successful canine styling salons, create the world's largest doggy day care company or become a successful speaker, author and influencer within the industry. The marketing principles that will get you there are the same across all sectors of the pet service industry.

How to use this book

This is a short book which I've split into three parts:

1. The launch and growth of a new pet business
2. Systemising, staffing and scaling your pet business
3. Expanding, innovating and re-inventing an established pet business

Sounds like a lot to cover in one short book, right?

Not really.

At each stage of your business journey there are surprisingly few 'fundamentals' you need to master to achieve success.

I'll be sharing the 'vital few' key business principles you must get right as you hit each stage of your pet business journey. In fact, you'll be learning just Seven of Dom's Golden Rules. Follow these rules and success will be yours.

You can, if you wish, skip ahead to the part which most applies to you, but it would be better for you to read the whole book in order, at least once. That way you'll see how the principles in each phase affect the next stage of your business growth.

As an example, if you are now full and have no space to take on new clients, you will likely feel like phase two is where you need to begin, but you'd be wrong. That's because before you take on staff, or even think about taking on a staff member, you should first make your business more profitable, by increasing your prices, and pricing is a topic in phase one in the next chapter.

So, as tempting as it is to skip forward, don't do it, or, if you do then be sure go back and re-read the whole book.

But my business is different!

Wrong, mon ami! Don't think that just because you are a dog trainer, a marketing example I give for groomers doesn't apply to you, or that a promotional tip for dog walkers has no relevance to your doggy day care business. It does.

Marketing is marketing is marketing, and by cross-referencing the ideas I share, you'll come up with unique ways to make your business stand out from the competition. It will also give you some ideas for how you can collaborate with other pet businesses in your town.

Treat this book like a manual. Underline and highlight light-bulb moments that leap out at you.

Why does this book matter to you?

Believe it or not, by just buying this book you've probably invested more money in your marketing education than most pet professionals invest in an entire lifetime.

Marketing and promotion seem to be dirty words for the fluffy bunny pet business owners who have a giant stick up their ass when it comes to making money from their business. That's because most of the 'average' pet business owners fall into the CPD trap of thinking they need to get better and better at 'the service' they provide.

Which is why 90% of the pet professionals out there have a hobby business which does nothing but pay for their 'seminar junkie' habit. If that sounds like you and you are happy to remain time and cash poor as your business does nothing but help swell the coffers of the dog training associations who are happy to take your money.

You'll see the same old faces there and you'll tell each other the same old stories about how difficult your business is, how shitty your clients are, and how empty your bank account is…

That's what average pet business owners do.

The key words there being 'average' and 'business owners'.

In order to make money from your pet business you need to treat it like a business. You need to be good at what you do for sure, and you should passionately care about the welfare of dogs, but I'm guessing you already tick those boxes.

For you, a profitable, proven pet business and marketing plan is what's needed.

Don't underestimate how important the marketing side of your business is.

You can attend a few courses and call yourself a dog walker, dog groomer or a dog trainer, but you'll only have a proper dog training, walking or grooming business, that makes a profit, with an effective marketing strategy.

I know lots of smart but stressed-out, talented but time-poor, skilful but skint pet business owners who have failed to grasp the importance of marketing, or they lack the discipline required to successfully promote their business.

Don't become one of the pissed-off pet professionals who foolishly fall under the counterfeit charms of fake social media gooroos, whose marketing advice consists of posting more and more updates on the ever-growing list of social media channels.

Facebook and Insta and Twitter, oh my!

Ask most pet business owners where they get their new clients from, and the answer will inevitably be 'word of mouth' and 'social media'.

'I couldn't run by business without social media.'

'Of course not,' I reply, 'because the concept of business didn't exist before 2004…'

Social media has its place, but it's just one of the 'online' tools you need to master, in addition to the 'offline' strategies that are generally far more effective and enjoyable ways for you to grow your business, and I'll be sharing the best of them with you in this book.

So, where do we start?

Well, as Maria von Trapp used to sing, 'We start at the very beginning, a very good place to start,' and when you turn the page we'll begin with phase one of launching and growing a pet business.

The fundamentals you learn in the next chapter will prevent you building your pet business on a house of sand and will give you the strong foundations you need for lasting success.

*Remember, you can get immediate access to the full audio version of this book by going to **www.petbusinessmarketing.com/magicgift***

Printed in Great Britain
by Amazon

59578050R00089